D1602430

BIGGER ISN'T NECESSARILY BETTER

BIGGER

ISN'T NECESSARILY

BETTER

LESSONS FROM THE HARVARD HOME BUILDER STUDY

FREDERICK ABERNATHY
KERMIT BAKER
KENT COLTON
DAVID WEIL

LEXINGTON BOOKS

Lanham • Boulder • New York • Toronto • Plymouth, UK

Published by Lexington Books
A wholly owned subsidiary of The Rowman & Littlefield Publishing Group, Inc.
4501 Forbes Boulevard, Suite 200, Lanham, Maryland 20706
www.lexingtonbooks.com

Estover Road, Plymouth PL6 7PY, United Kingdom

British Library Cataloguing in Publication Information Available

Library of Congress Cataloging-in-Publication Data available

ISBN 978-0-7391-7288-9 (cloth : alk. paper)
ISBN 978-0-7391-7289-6 (pbk. : alk. paper)
ISBN 978-0-7391-7290-2 (electronic)

Printed in the United States of America

CONTENTS

PREFACE

In 2001 Frederick H. Abernathy and David Weil, along with John T. Dunlop and Janice H. Hammond, had just completed a decade-long study of the textile and apparel industry, examining how consolidation had led to streamlined supply chains and greater efficiencies throughout the system. Their book, *A Stitch in Time—Lean Retailing and the Transformation of Manufacturing,* documented the ways that the retailing industry had changed as the result of better information processing systems to track product production, inventories, and sales.

At the time, the residential construction industry had undergone its own consolidation, providing large-scale home builders better access to capital to fund their operations, the ability to secure prime land positions, and greater market power in negotiations with product manufacturers and dealers. Among other things, growth in home builders' scale of operations was expected to produce greater efficiencies in the residential construction supply chain and building processes.

Abernathy and Weil approached Harvard's Joint Center for Housing Studies about studying how the emergence of large home building companies was changing, and would continue to change, industry practices. The center's research staff, along with its Policy Advisory Board (PAB) member companies—including national building product suppliers, distributors, and major home builders—agreed to this proposal and the Harvard Home Builder Study was launched in 2001.

Before undertaking a study of how scale gains were reshaping home builder operations, however, the study team looked at how the building products supply chain was responding to home builder consolidation. This analysis, known as the Harvard Building Products Distribution Study, revealed that professional dealers were shifting their product and service mix to attract high-volume builders (Abernathy et al. 2004). By focusing on builders that purchased materials for at least 500 homes a year, pro dealers could follow the lead of major building product retailers such as The Home Depot and Lowe's to use their emerging economies of scale to shorten the distribution chain and reduce product costs.

Once it was clear how the building products supply chain was evolving, a more direct examination of the benefits of home builder consolidation could begin. The focus of this phase of the research was not to question *if* bigger was better for home builders, but rather to determine *how* it was better. Because of economies of scale and increased market power, large-scale builders enjoyed several potential advantages over their smaller competitors. In essence, the research goal was to evaluate how the principal operational benefits conferred by size—including improved ability to manage risk, streamline supply chains, and coordinate labor—contributed to large home builders' financial success.

An in-depth survey exploring these topics was conducted in 2005 in the midst of one of the strongest housing market expansions in generations. However, by the time the study team analyzed the survey results, US housing market conditions had changed significantly and were headed into a major downturn. Single-family housing starts, which had been running at an annual rate of 1.0–1.2 million in the mid- to late 1990s, began accelerating in early 2002 and peaked above 1.7 million in the first quarter of 2006. But by the first quarter of 2009, single-family starts had fallen below 360,000 at an annual rate—a drop of nearly 80 percent from the high. This placed the downturn as the deepest in over 60 years and added another significant dimension to the analysis.

While the dramatic housing bust obviously complicated the analysis, it also increased the importance of understanding how large home builders used their scale to become more efficient during the boom years. In fact, the survey revealed that most major builders did not capture many of the operational benefits of consolidation during one of the strongest market upturns in several generations. Instead, their attention was focused on acquiring land and resources in those markets with rapidly appreciating home prices. Less attention was paid to the cost side of the ledger or to practices that might improve builders' ability to respond to changes in consumer demand.

Yet the rapidly deteriorating housing market underscored the pressing need for builders to handle ongoing demand-side risk more effectively in the future through operational innovations. Examining the experience of companies in other industries that had grappled with volatile demand risks—from autos to computers to retailing—provided insights into how builders might better cope with these challenges going forward.

At the peak of the last boom, with their steady access to capital and techniques designed to manage the inevitable ups and downs of the industry, many companies felt that they had mastered the cyclical nature of home building. Yet they soon found their companies falling off the tallest precipice in housing industry history as the market collapsed around them. We believe that as the home building sector slowly recovers, it has never been more important to understand what did—and did not—happen in the last boom. Only then can we expect the next generation of builders to fully leverage the potential arising from scale.

The authors thank the Alfred P. Sloan Foundation, the Joint Center for Housing Studies of Harvard University, and the National Housing Endowment for their generous financial support of this project. Many individuals provided critical assistance for this effort. At the Joint Center, Bill Apgar and Eric Belsky offered helpful insights about the operations of the housing market. Rachel Roth provided able research assistance with the Harvard Building Products Distribution Study, and Becky Russell and Tyler Johnston with the early stages of the Harvard Home Builder Study. We are particularly grateful to Abbe Will, who provided superb support beyond the call of duty for the Harvard Home Builder Study in the final stages of the project. Marina Di Donato-McLaughlin provided ongoing administrative support throughout the project. We also thank Marcia Fernald for her careful editing of the final manuscript and John Skurchak for his work on graphic design.

Barbara Alexander, formerly of UBS and a Fellow of the Joint Center, ably formed and coordinated a Joint Center Advisory Panel of principals of major firms in the home building industry (see Appendix A for member names and affiliations). The panel had the important role of insuring that the survey appropriately explored the processes and procedures of home building during industry consolidation and expansion in 1999–2004. The questionnaire evolved into one for the corporate office and a separate one for operating divisions. The two questionnaires are available for downloading at both www.jchs.harvard.edu/ and www.hctar.org/. We are also very grateful to the individual members of the Joint Center's Policy Advisory Board and others in the industry who provided insights and reviewed several drafts of the survey.

The Joint Center Advisory Panel was also critical in insuring broad industry participation in the survey. Members worked hard to encourage home building firms of all sizes to participate in the surveys that led to this book.

This book would not have been possible without the active participation of the survey respondents: 41 home builders who answered the extensive corporate questionnaire and encouraged several of their divisions to respond to a much longer and highly detailed survey, yielding a set of 88 unique divisional responses. The companies answering the surveys ranged in size from builders selling fewer than 500 homes in 2004 to national corporations selling more than 10,000 homes that year. They were promised anonymity if they participated, so we can only thank them without attribution for their immense contribution.

Finally, the late John T. Dunlop was an active participant in this research effort at its early stages. Each of the authors wishes to acknowledge the guidance and debt of gratitude owed to this remarkable person—a distinguished labor economist, academic administrator, US Secretary of Labor, mentor of many, and a man of uncommon integrity and wisdom.

1

HOME BUILDING—IS BIGGER BETTER?

Much has been—and remains to be—written about how lenders, risky financial instruments, heedless consumers, and lax regulation all contributed to the spectacular US housing boom and bust.[1] Yet in unraveling what happened, housing industry critics and defenders alike have paid little attention to how home builders were operating during the boom years of the late 1990s and early 2000s.

Understanding what did and did not happen on the residential construction side during that period is the central focus of this book. After years of industry consolidation, several home building companies had become national in scope, selling as many as 50,000 houses annually in locations across the country. Riding the wave of soaring house prices and falling borrowing costs, these large firms saw their profit margins climb higher and higher while paying scant attention to the efficiency of their home building operations. Indeed, at the peak of the boom, many large home builders felt that they had finally mastered the cyclical nature of their business and learned how to manage the inevitable ups and downs of construction activity. Soon enough, however, they found themselves in the deepest abyss in industry history. Bigger, it turned out, was not necessarily better in terms of managing onsite practices.

The Harvard Home Builder Survey was launched just before the 2005 peak in the US housing market. At that time, the goal was to examine how—rather than *if*—industry concentration was leading to greater efficiency. The expectation was that, like personal computers, automobiles, retailing, and other concentrated industries, large home builders would take advantage of their scale to develop best practices in a variety of areas, from managing the construction process and coordinating subcontractors, to streamlining their supply chains, to leveraging the power of new information and communication technology.

---

1   For just a few examples, see Michael Lewis, *The Big Short* (2010); Andrew Ross Sorkin, *Too Big To Fail* (2009); Daniel Immergluck, *Foreclosed* (2009); Charles R. Morris, *The Trillion Dollar Meltdown* (2008); Robert J. Shiller, *The Subprime Solution* (2008); William Cohan, *House of Cards* (2009); Bethany McLean and Joe Nocera, *All the Devils Are Here* (2010); and Mark Zandi, *Financial Shock* (2009).

As the following pages reveal, this was hardly the case. While wildly profitable during the boom years, large home builders typically were not focused on local operations—especially in markets where house prices were skyrocketing. Now, in the aftermath of the massive housing market bust, improving the efficiency of their operations provides a clear opportunity for home builders to prosper in the years ahead.

THE HOME BUILDING BOOM

The single-family housing industry has generally been one of expansion followed by contraction, mimicking the business cycle or, as in the current recession, a leading indicator of a downturn in business activity. Following the recovery from the recession that accompanied the bursting of the dot-com bubble, single-family home starts climbed rapidly from 1.2 million in 2000 to a remarkable peak of 1.7 million units in 2005 **(Figure 1.1)**. The National Association of Home Builders (NAHB), in an effort to measure the importance of home building to the economy, estimated that the total contribution of residential investment and housing services to gross domestic product (GDP) grew from 16.6 percent in 2000 to more than 18.7 percent in 2005.[2]

FIGURE 1.1

Single-Family Construction Surged from 2000 to 2005

New privately owned single-family housing units started (millions)

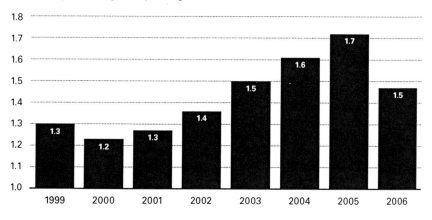

Source: US Census Bureau, Survey of Construction, 2011a.

Population growth in Japan and many European countries has been stagnant or decreasing, leading to weak demand for new housing. In contrast, the US population has continued to expand over time. The US Census Bureau estimated the population grew from 279 million in 1999 to almost 293 million in 2004 (the years covered in

---

2   The NAHB's Michael Carliner, in an October 2001 article in *Housing Economics*, explained the breakdown of home building's contribution to the economy in 2000. For more up-to-date information, see Grist 2010.

the Harvard Home Builder Survey), representing an increase of over 2.73 million individuals per year on average. Annual population growth by itself, however, does not directly lead to increased demand for new housing; it is the translation of population growth into new households that is an important driver of additional housing demand.[3] The Census Bureau (2010) estimated that the number of US households rose from 103.9 million in 1999 to 112.0 million in 2004, with annual growth averaging 1.62 million new households.

Along with household formation, US housing demand was also driven by growth of GDP. The US Department of Commerce (2011) estimated that GDP (in chained 2005 dollars) grew from a $10.7 trillion seasonally adjusted annual rate in April 1999 to about $12.2 trillion in April 2004. In other words, GDP expanded 14 percent during this five-year period. The strong growth in GDP not only contributed to the surge in single-family housing starts from 1999 to 2004, but also increased demand for consumer products in general.

Increases in households and family income have been important elements in prior residential building booms. As is now well known, the early-2000s boom was also accompanied by developments in the capital markets. The expansion of home building was fueled by a long period of low interest rates maintained by the Federal Reserve to stimulate recovery from the earlier dot-com recession. These policies also drove down home mortgage interest rates. At the same time, the collateralization of mortgage securities drastically expanded the pool of investors willing to lend for mortgages. In particular, the invention of new forms of adjustable-rate loans and the dramatic expansion of the subprime market led to unprecedented flows of capital available for lending.

Subprime lending increased over a much longer period than just the Harvard Home Builder Survey years of 1999–2004. From 1990 to 2006, subprime lending soared from an estimated $37 billion, or 8.1 percent of all one- to four-family mortgage originations, to $600 billion, or 20.1 percent of originations (Inside Mortgage Finance 2009; see also, Gerardi, Shapiro, and Willen 2007). Somewhat lost in the ongoing discussion of the mortgage market debacle is the fact that subprime loans and other higher-priced instruments created an opportunity for homeownership to people long excluded from those markets. As noted by the late Edward Gramlich, a member of the Board of Governors of the Federal Reserve (and an early predictor of the broader impacts of a subprime meltdown), "The subprime mortgage market was a valid innovation, and it did enable 12 million households to become homeowners, a large majority of these who would have been denied mortgage credit in the early 1990s" (2007, p. 107).

Of course, as has become abundantly clear, the seemingly unquenchable thirst for securitized mortgage investments created an environment in which banks, other lending institutions, and mortgage brokers in particular lent money to prospective and current homeowners with little ability to take on those debt obligations. As the

---

3   Housing demand includes not only owner-occupied single-family homes but also multifamily housing, rental units of all types, and vacation homes.

subprime market reached its peak, loan arrangements allowing borrowers to simply state their current income and provide no verification of employment became common, as did mortgages allowing for interest-only payments. By 2005, the combination of these factors led to the dramatic expansion of the domestic housing stock and unsustainable level of construction activity. The Group of 20 summarized the confluence of factors in 2008 in its *Declaration of the Summit on Financial Markets and the World Economy:*

> During a period of strong global growth, growing capital flows, and prolonged stability earlier this decade, market participants sought higher yields without an adequate appreciation of the risks and failed to exercise proper due diligence. At the same time, weak underwriting standards, unsound risk management practices, increasingly complex and opaque financial products, and consequent excessive leverage combined to create vulnerabilities in the system. Policy-makers, regulators and supervisors, in some advanced countries, did not adequately appreciate and address the risks building up in financial markets, keep pace with financial innovation, or take into account the systemic ramifications of domestic regulatory actions (p. 1).

The rapid expansion of housing was accompanied by an even more rapid increase in home prices in many markets across the country. But Alan Greenspan, then Chairman of the Federal Reserve, dismissed the idea of a developing housing bubble in a speech in October 2004.[4] In that speech, Chairman Greenspan said: "While local economies may experience significant speculative price imbalances, a national severe price distortion seems most unlikely."

It is certainly true that the housing expansion and rise in existing home values were far from uniform across the country. Housing demand was very strong in a number of metropolitan areas, accompanied by high levels of home appreciation or a speculative price rise in accord with Chairman Greenspan's remarks. In other regions of the country, demand for new housing was moderate, with similarly moderate levels of home price appreciation that indicated a better balance between housing supply and demand.

The home builders benefiting from the construction boom were also unevenly distributed—not only by location, but also by size. In particular, the industry had consolidated after the national economic recession in the early 1990s, with the top 10 national builders accounting for over 20 percent of new residential construction in 2004. However, the forces leading to builder consolidation originated well before the 1990–1 downturn.

THE SEEDS OF CONSOLIDATION

Until the 1970s, savings and loan institutions (S&Ls), along with local savings banks, were the dominant source of both mortgage loans to homebuyers and financing for developers' land purchases and construction costs. The capital base of S&Ls was principally short-term deposits in the form of savings and checking accounts, while

---

4   The speech received modest coverage until after the bursting of the housing bubble, when columnist Paul Krugman quoted Greenspan's remark in the *New York Times* on August 29, 2005.

loans to homebuyers were generally long-term fixed-rate mortgages. This "borrow short/lend long" strategy created a difficult environment for the thrift industry. When inflation soared following the OPEC oil embargo in the mid-1970s, these institutions had to pay depositors higher interest rates to attract deposits. At the same time, receipts from their older fixed-rate mortgage loans became increasingly inadequate to balance their operations. By late in the decade, it became apparent that the S&Ls were overextended. As a Congressional Budget Office study (1993) put it:

> The rigid regulatory design of the thrift industry, which limited the types of investments thrifts could make and the rates they could pay on deposits, left the industry extremely vulnerable to the high and volatile interest rates of the late 1970s and early 1980s. To be competitive, thrifts were forced to pay higher rates on their deposits than they could earn on their assets. The resulting mismatch in the maturities of thrifts' assets and liabilities almost wiped out the market value of the industry's net worth (p. xi).

Financial deregulation in the early 1980s only compounded the problem, allowing institutions to make riskier loans—often for commercial real estate where they had little expertise. Again, according to the same CBO report:

> Moreover, it was a mistake to grant more liberal investment powers to undercapitalized institutions and relax other regulations that fostered safety and soundness in thrifts' operations. In this lax regulatory environment, many owners, managers, and directors of unhealthy thrifts speculated with or plundered the funds of their institutions (p. xi).

The net result was that nearly 750 institutions failed during the early 1990s recession, and many others ceased lending to builders or homebuyers. The severe credit crunch forced home builders to turn to Wall Street for capital in the belief that equity financing would provide a better way to deal with the cyclical nature of their industry.

For the typical small-scale builder, however, going public was not an option. To access this source of capital, firms needed to expand their scale of operations. Given the limits to organic growth that builders could reasonably achieve, acquisitions thus became a key business strategy. Purchasing companies in markets a particular builder did not currently serve was often the most effective path to growth. In general, the land holdings of acquired builders were their most valuable asset in that the acquiring company could increase production faster than if it had to go through the time-consuming land purchase and entitlement process.

Home builder consolidation was thus motivated less by the desire for scale per se than to attract sufficient interest from Wall Street investors to secure the capital necessary to develop favorable land positions. Access to capital became increasingly important in subsequent years in order to finance larger and larger land holdings, which builders acknowledged were critical to their success.

THE GROWING DOMINANCE OF BIG BUILDERS
The strongest housing market expansion since World War II set the stage for the large home builders to achieve dramatic increases in market share. According to

industry data, the nation's top 10 home builders expanded their market share from 9.7 percent in 1994 to more than 21 percent in 2004 **(Figure 1.2)**. While a dramatic increase for home builders, this gain was fairly modest by the standards of other consolidated industries such as banking, automobiles, and even manufacturing and distribution within the residential construction industry.

FIGURE 1.2

The Top 10 Home Builders More than Doubled Their Market Share Between 1994 and 2004

Share of new single-family homes built for sale by top 10 US home builders (percent)

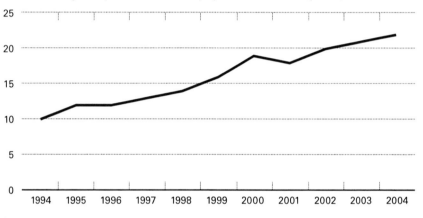

Sources: Authors' tabulations of *Builder* magazine's annual "Builder 100" list; US Census Bureau, Survey of Construction, 2011b.

Acquisitions allowed major home builders to greatly exceed the market share that they would otherwise have been able to achieve through internal growth. Indeed, according to NAHB's Carliner (2005), the top 10 market share would have increased to only about 11 percent over this period if they had relied solely on organic growth of their 1994 holdings **(Figure 1.3)**.

FIGURE 1.3

Builder Growth Was Driven Primarily by Acquisitions

Share of single-family homes completed for sale by top 10 US home builders (percent)

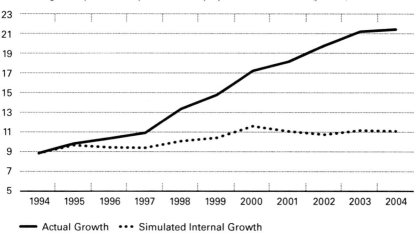

—— Actual Growth • • • Simulated Internal Growth

Source: Carliner 2005.

These large companies also posted impressive growth in revenue and housing production. For example, when Beazer Homes went public in 1994, the company sold just 4,000 homes and took in $540 million in revenue. By 2003, Beazer reported over 15,000 home closings and annual revenues of $3.2 billion. Similarly, D.R. Horton became a public company in 1992. Between that year and 2003, its home closings increased from 1,200 to almost 36,000 while revenues climbed from $180 million to $8.7 billion. Home builder concentration at the metropolitan level was even more intense **(Figure 1.4)**. For example, the top five builders in Las Vegas, Houston, Dallas, Orlando and Phoenix accounted for more than 30 percent of all homes sold within these markets in 2004.

FIGURE 1.4

Big Builders Captured Even Larger Shares Within Metro Markets
Top 5 builder share of permits in top 10 markets by 2004 construction levels (percent)

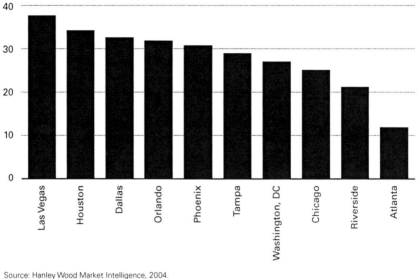

Source: Hanley Wood Market Intelligence, 2004.

CONVENTIONAL WISDOM ABOUT SCALE
Several industry analysts presented an extensive list of reasons why consolidation should benefit larger home builders both financially and operationally (see, for example, DeCain 2002 and Whelan 2005). The most ambitious study, *The Impending Consolidation of the Homebuilding Industry* published by Andersen Corporate Finance in 2002, made several predictions about the competitive advantages of larger publicly traded companies. Specifically, large home builders should see:

- **Lower capital costs.** The report states that large publicly traded builders typically had a 125 basis-point advantage on debt. Equity advantages are more complex to estimate because they are based on perceived risk. The report indicates that equity capital costs for public builders were 10–15 percent, compared with 20–25 percent for private builders. For a $200 million company that is 50 percent leveraged, Andersen estimated the annual benefit of equity financing was $5 million. In effect, however, the benefit was that public builders could choose between debt and equity financing depending on market conditions, while private builders were largely confined to debt financing—a serious constraint when financial markets collapsed.

- **Lower operating and overhead costs.** Lower-cost supplier agreements and the ability to draw on cash reserves to buy less expensive land during downturns gave large public builders an estimated 200 basis-point advantage. For that same $200 million company, this translated into a $10 million benefit.

- **Increased revenue enhancements.** Large national builders should enjoy significantly stronger revenues through branding. Companies that are not large enough to develop brand identities, in contrast, would likely face declining prospects.

- **Land advantages.** Only the largest builders would be able to control substantial land positions, while smaller builders would lack the resources to option significant land for long periods.

This 2002 Andersen study thus predicted that by 2011, the top 20 US home builders would account for 75 percent of new home sales, while the nation's largest builder could have a 20 percent market share. While these predictions are well off the mark, the housing market downturn beginning in 2006 clearly played a role in limiting the benefits of consolidation in recent years.

Meanwhile, Harvard Business School's Michael Porter made one of the few attempts to empirically study the relationship between home builder size and profitability. Using 2002 data collected by *Professional Builder* magazine on the 400 largest US home builders, Porter's analysis (2003) showed that the 20 largest companies had higher gross margins, lower selling and general administration costs, and lower financing rates. As a result, this group of companies had higher profit margins than the rest of the top 400 builders.

Porter also presented evidence that large builders had lower building materials costs, at least in part because they were more likely to buy products directly from manufacturers. Their construction labor costs were also lower, and they had better access to capital than smaller builders. Better access to capital, in turn, gave larger builders better access to land because they had more "patient" capital to wait out land entitlement delays in heavily regulated markets.

Nevertheless, Porter did not fully connect the dots between lower materials, labor, and capital costs and higher profitability. Do lower input costs fall directly to the bottom line, or do they enable builders to put more resources into improving their efficiency (e.g., reducing construction cycle times and lowering production costs)? Do their superior land positions and access to capital allow larger builders to operate in markets where margins are greater, independent of their operating performance? Porter instead argued that the emerging structure of the home building industry, driven by consolidation, would ensure that larger builders had inherent competitive advantages that would enable them to outperform smaller players.

Research conducted under the Partnership for Advancing Technology in Housing (PATH) program, funded by the US Department of Housing and Urban Development (HUD), did find that larger builders made operational changes to improve their profitability. For example, a PATH-funded study by the Center for Housing Research at Virginia Tech (Koebel and Cavell 2006) concluded that larger home builders were more innovative than smaller companies. In addition, they found that decentralization within a large home building company contributed to innovation at the division level. Moreover, large-scale builders with aggressive growth plans included information technology innovation as one element in their strategy to increase market share and profitability.

In contrast to the research extolling the benefits of consolidation among US companies, a study of the British home building industry came to very different conclusions about the motivations for a similar wave of consolidation in that country. In an exhaustive review of 20th century British home builders, Fred Wellings (2006) reviewed several common reasons offered for industry consolidation, including access to capital; ability to control large development sites; technological change and innovation; scale requirements for marketing; and scale benefits for product purchasing.

After carefully reviewing each of these motivations, Wellings rejected the idea that the increased size of home building firms provides significant advantages for any of these functions. Indeed, in an analysis of 76 British home builders producing 50 to 15,000 housing units in 2001, he found no relationship between company profit margins and scale of operations.[5] Concerned that 2001 might have been an atypical year, Wellings replicated the analysis for 1987, 2000, and 2004, and again found virtually no relationship between size of company and profitability.[6] Also testing whether this relationship might hold only for larger firms, he restricted the 2001 analysis to companies building 500–5,000 units and then to companies building 1,000–5,000. In both analyses, no meaningful relationship could be identified between builder size and profit (Wellings 2006, 168–71).

Rather than the necessities of scale economies in the industry, Wellings suggests three other potential motivations for the increase in home builder consolidation in the UK: financial market pressures, with the stock market playing a key role in facilitating acquisitions and in demanding growth from these companies; personal ambition that motivated businessmen to seek growth and size for their own sake; and overexpansion by some home builders ahead of a major downturn, creating opportunities for surviving firms during the next upturn.

THE VIRTUOUS CIRCLE HYPOTHESIS

In many sectors of the economy, a feedback loop of positive advantages normally follows industry consolidation: firms with larger market share benefit from increased scale economies which, in turn, lead to performance improvements and further increases in market share. A similar feedback logic could be expected to prevail in the home building industry given its consolidation. Market concentration gives rise to scale, and scale conveys market power in negotiations with suppliers and subcontractors and more advantageous cost positions relative to smaller competitors. In addition, larger builders can reinvest in their operations and adopt best practices that enable them to produce homes more quickly and at lower cost. Investment in innovative operating practices in turn allows larger companies to outperform their smaller competitors. This success leads to further consolidation, more potential scale advantages, and more access to capital to reinvest in operations to achieve even

---

5 Wellings found that builder scale could explain less than one percent of the variation in profit margins. Specifically, he reported an R^2 of 0.0014 in his profitability models (p. 168).

6 The variation in operating profits explained by builder size had an R^2 of 0.008 in 1987, 0.004 in 2000, and 0.003 in 2004.

greater efficiencies and improved performance, and so on. The predicted virtuous circle reinforces itself, leading to even greater consolidation **(Figure 1.5)**.

FIGURE 1.5

The Virtuous Circle Hypothesis Predicts that Big Home Builders Would Set Best Practices for the Industry

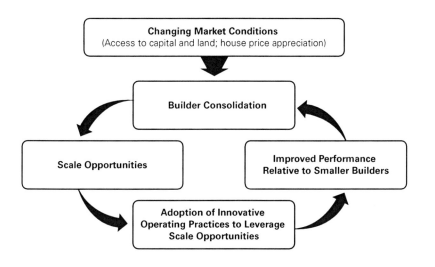

Virtuous circles that translate scale into innovation and efficiency and then back again into scale have emerged in other major industries. For example, consolidation of automotive manufacturers and the resulting scale opportunities have been a key element in unit cost reductions and improved financial performance. In the early days of the industry, there were numerous small and relatively inefficient manufacturers. Henry Ford's assembly lines allowed the mass production of cars, which in turn produced greater labor efficiencies and presented scale opportunities, which in turn allowed reinvestment of more resources in operations, producing even greater production efficiencies. Similarly in the computer industry, as manufacturers such as Dell Computer increased their sales volumes, they improved their capacity to assemble components from suppliers around the world, reduced the prices they paid for those components, and ratcheted down the costs of logistics for moving parts and final merchandise by improving operational efficiency. Although consolidation may have occurred for different reasons in home building than in other industries (i.e., access to new markets, land acquisition, and building brand awareness), large-scale companies should have been able to capture similar benefits from scale.

The Harvard Home Builder Study was formulated with the virtuous circle hypothesis in mind. While consolidation provided builders with access to capital for acquisitions as well as for expanding their land positions, it should in principle also provide larger companies—regardless of the markets they served—both the incentives and resources to implement efficient operating practices such as:

- negotiating lower prices and/or better service from suppliers;

- modifying subcontractor relationships in terms of bidding of work, management at the job site, purchase of materials, and overall construction coordination;

- eliminating supply chain redundancies and streamlining the processes to plan, acquire, and transport building supplies to the job site; and

- improving management and coordination of internal and external operations by investing in the new generation of information and communication technology.

In practice, large home builders did take advantage of their growing scale to access capital markets, take aggressive—and during the housing boom, very profitable—land positions, and build brand awareness. However, they failed to take full advantage of their scale to seize the opportunity to implement the advanced operating practices noted above.

While some builders did in fact adopt advanced practices during this period, implementation of those practices related less to company size than to the nature of the markets in which the builders competed. Indeed, local house price appreciation is a far better predictor of which home builders improved their operating performance during the boom years and which did not. In markets where builders were forced to compete, they did improve their operating performance. This finding is related to a fundamental aspect of home building. Although some builders became national in scope as they grew, merged, and went public, their day-to-day operations remained highly local and decentralized. This, as we shall see, has profound implications.

ORGANIZATION OF THE BOOK

The Harvard Home Builder Study examines how large home builders performed the many activities involved in the business of residential construction, from land purchase and development to on-site coordination of workers and management of materials. The following chapters are structured around those sets of practices.

- **Chapter 2** explains some of the challenges involved in designing the Harvard Home Builder Study and lays out the central research questions in detail. This section also provides a brief description of the survey and the home building companies that participated in the process.

- **Chapter 3** presents the corporate-level results of the Harvard Home Builder Survey related to financial performance and what companies saw as the sources of their profitability. In particular, this chapter describes how large builders were able to take advantage of their growing scale to access capital markets, take aggressive land positions, and build brand awareness.

- **Chapter 4** examines labor practices at the jobsite. After describing the distinctive way that large-scale home builders manage construction, the chapter analyzes how scale, market characteristics, and other factors affect the coordination of subcontractors as well as the actual construction of homes.

- **Chapter 5** focuses on advanced operational practices, including supply chain management, use of preassembled components, and supplier installation. Builders have the potential to construct homes faster and less expensively using more efficient assembly processes, and this chapter analyzes the extent to which builders took advantage of this opportunity.

- **Chapter 6** explores the role that information and communications technology (ICT) played in helping large home builders coordinate key activities, from estimating construction costs to keeping subcontractors and suppliers on top of schedules. The chapter reveals which builders were particularly advanced in their use of technology to manage their operations.

- **Chapter 7** summarizes the key results of the Harvard Home Builder Study and explains the significant impediments that limit adoption of innovative home building practices.

- **Chapter 8** then turns to the lessons to be learned from the experience of other consolidated industries to better position home builders and their stakeholders for a prosperous future.

The United States faces very different housing market conditions now than when the Harvard Home Builder Survey was conducted. We believe that the time has never been more important to fully understand what did and did not happen during the past boom. Much has and is being written on the effects of lending practices, demographics, consumer preferences, and Wall Street on that boom. We believe that little light, however, has been shed on what home builders actually did in terms of their practices on the ground during this period. But a revival of the housing sector will rely on substantial innovation on the operational side of the business, requiring home builders to learn lessons from other industries that have transformed themselves after crises. Given the central role that home building plays in our economy, we all share an interest in the prospects for fundamental transformation of this vital sector.

2

STUDYING THE HOME BUILDING INDUSTRY

Analyzing the operations of large-scale home builders poses a number of research complexities. Housing construction is as distinctive and multifaceted as, say, automobile production. But analysts studying auto manufacturing can go to factories to observe each step in the assembly process, compare the procedures of major firms, and determine best practices for the industry. Home building, in contrast, occurs at tens of thousands of sites all over the country. The industry also includes a vast array of firms that range from large, sophisticated, and heavily capitalized corporations with divisions nationwide to individual contractors focused on a single market and with limited resources. Moreover, the product itself can be of almost any size and configuration, from a multimillion-dollar mansion to a modest house designed for a first-time buyer.

Yet another complication is that many factors other than home builder size affect business outcomes. During the period from 1999 to 2004, the industry was not only transformed by consolidation and unusually favorable housing market conditions, but also by unique circumstances in specific markets, including meteoric house price appreciation in certain areas. These and other complex forces confound the relationship between company scale and performance.

The Harvard Home Builder Study is based on what is perhaps the most extensive survey of large home builders ever conducted. A sample of companies building at least 500 homes in 2004 was asked to document their operations in the previous five years, with the goal of measuring how innovative practices contributed to their strong financial performance. Companies of that size might reasonably be expected to benefit from scale and therefore adopt some innovative practices. The practices under consideration relate to land management, planning and coordination with subcontractors, use of preassembly and supplier installation, supply chain management, and use of information and communication technology.

This chapter first outlines the sequence of steps involved in home building, which provided the basic framework for the survey. The next section explains why the investigation of best practices focused on production of entry-level homes. The chapter then provides a brief overview of the survey and the rationale behind its structure. The following section describes the role of local market conditions in determining the benefits of home builder size, and explains the measurement of market competitiveness. The final two sections provide a brief overview of the companies participating in the Harvard Home Builder Study and of the scope and structure of the survey.

BUILDING THE MACHINE FOR LIVING

The great French architect Le Corbusier (1887–1965) famously described a home this way: "A house is a machine for living." Many in the contemporary world would find Le Corbusier-designed homes—ascetic, spare, rectangular structures of brick and stone, with an open floor plan—difficult places to live. But the central concern of this research is not the design of homes but rather the actual process of construction.

Building a shelter—housing—is a fundamental human activity that has been going on from the beginning of time; it is second in importance only to the gathering of food. Given the vital nature of this basic human activity, one would expect it to be exhaustively studied. But this is hardly the case. Most major US universities have schools of architecture/design teaching future home designers the fundamentals of modern building design and construction. Few look at the complex set of underlying activities required to build a home. When not focused on design, studies of home building generally look at the cost of a typical home, the number of square feet, the number of bathrooms, etc., as well as the distribution of costs to labor and materials. They generally do not look into the land acquisition and development strategy; the organization and efficiency of the building trades; the use of advanced computer software programs and the Internet to coordinate construction; the use of preassembled components; and the details of building products supply chains.

To examine the activities of home builders, it is therefore necessary to understand what it takes to build the "machine for living." To begin with, however, it is important to note that much of the work in constructing homes occurs locally. While one reason for this is the difficulty of transporting major components over long distances, local building codes are also an important constraint. Given that codes can vary significantly by jurisdiction, a home that complies with regulations in one location might not comply in another. Despite this challenge, large home builders operating in several markets should still enjoy certain scale advantages over smaller competitors.

The first step in the home building process is to acquire land. Once land assembly is complete, the parcel is subdivided into buildable lots. Builders must secure permits from local authorities to make site improvements such as roads, storm water drains, and utilities, as well as go through architectural, engineering, environmental, and code compliance reviews.

The frame of a house is erected on a foundation, either a poured concrete slab or a basement. The frame is made with load-bearing panels constructed from 2x4-inch vertical studs, 16 inches on center. The panels are either built on site or trucked in from a plant where they are made. They are generally sheathed on the outside with plywood or OSB (oriented strand board), and then wrapped with a film to make the frame wind-tight and ready for siding. The panels are linked together to form the perimeter of the house and set the dimensions of individual rooms.

An off-site supplier usually provides roof trusses, made from 2x4s, as a subassembly. The trusses are covered with plywood decking and made weather-tight with roofing felt and shingles. Windows are another subassembly purchased directly from the manufacturer or dealer/distributor. After the house is weather-tight, electrical work, plumbing, insulation, and HVAC systems can be roughed in. Then comes drywall and finish work—including carpentry, plumbing and bath connection, kitchen cabinets and counters, painting, and carpets.

Rather than a single company, numerous contractors perform the many activities involved in construction. One set of contractors—sometimes called basic trades—is present at most stages of the process. Basic trade contractors undertake initial steps such as framing the house once the slab has been prepared; mid-term steps such as installation of windows and wallboard; and final steps such as finish carpentry, including installation of cabinets, molding, exterior finishes, and doors. Other sets of contractors—specialty trades—are involved at specific points in the construction project to install systems (such as electrical, plumbing, and HVAC) or finish portions of the house (tiling, brickwork, or roofing). These contractors are usually independent of one another, and may either work directly for a lead contractor or act as subcontractors for other contractors on site.

Materials for each of these construction stages must be selected, purchased, and brought to the site in a timely manner. The parties doing so may be the home builder, a lead contractor, subcontractors, or a third-party provider such as a specialty products supplier or building materials manufacturer. More likely, some combination of several of these players provides the materials for construction.

The highly complex and dynamic nature of housing production arises from the myriad individuals and companies involved in the separate but deeply interconnected steps (whether they occur sequentially or in tandem) of the construction process. The challenge facing home builders is not only coordinating multiple activities effectively, but also operating within the particular zoning requirements of the local area, coordinating local and regional markets for contractors and labor, and adhering to the design, cost, scheduling, and quality standards specified by the corporate office.

FOCUS ON ENTRY-LEVEL HOMES

Major companies often hone their production strategies for the market segments with the strongest consumer demand. These often turn out to be entry-level products. The auto industry, for example, developed its best practices for assembly for models like the Toyota Corolla, the Ford Focus, or the Chevrolet Aveo rather than on high-end models with relatively small markets.

A similar story can be found in the retail industry. In the early 1990s, mass merchant retailers like Walmart and department stores like Dillard's and Federated developed modern "lean retailing" practices that use information technologies and advanced logistics to limit their inventory risk by focusing on products with high demand volumes and limited fashion content, such as underwear, jeans, and t-shirts. Expansion of lean retailing practices to more fashion-oriented products came well after they had been applied broadly to basic apparel items (Abernathy et al. 1999).

Like autos and apparel, single-family homes come in a vast array of sizes and sell at widely different price points. At one extreme are homes akin to high-end automobiles like Rolls Royce or pricey couture fashions produced in small lots. For example, the *New York Times* reported in 2007 that Saudi Arabia's Prince Bandar bin Sultan was offering his single-family vacation home in Aspen, Colorado, for sale at $135 million. At 55,000 square feet and situated on 95 acres of land, the property is clearly not a home where efficiency of assembly was a design or construction concern.

At the other end of the spectrum are the starter homes intended for households first entering the owner market. Customers for these entry-level homes—like consumers of entry-level cars and basic apparel items—demand products that provide the essentials without luxury or fashion touches and at an affordable price. To be profitable, builders of entry-level cars and entry-level homes must design and assemble attractive products efficiently and quickly, using their very best techniques. Although entry-level homes still vary in design and price across local markets, they provide the most useful benchmark for comparing home builder practices.

Entry-level homes are a useful focus for analysis for additional reasons. Major home builders are usually organized into a number of operating divisions, each generally building in a single metropolitan area. A typical division builds several different models and is responsible for all phases of the process, beginning with buying and entitling land and securing permits from local governments through the actual construction of homes.

A typical large home builder may construct different types of housing in the markets it serves. In some areas, the company may focus on building "tradeup" homes designed for growing families with rising household incomes. In others, it may produce houses for retired couples with no children living at home, often in age-restricted communities.

Almost all the home builders participating in the Harvard Home Builder Study, however, built entry-level homes in at least some of the markets where they competed. Starter homes are usually marketed to single individuals, young couples, or young families for whom cost is paramount. Building for this market segment thus makes production efficiency and cost management critical. The Harvard Home Builder Survey therefore focused specifically on practices related to starter homes because operating efficiencies deriving from scale would be easier to identify.

In recent years, starter homes generally have been built at the metropolitan edge where large tracts of land are available for subdivision and where land prices are affordable. A rough rule of thumb is that a finished home might sell for three to four times the underlying land costs: the higher the lot cost, the lower the multiple for the finished home and land. As a result, starter homes in different areas of the country have vastly different selling prices depending on the cost of entitled land.

While the basic layout of entry-level homes is generally similar, amenities may differ depending on market conditions and buyer expectations. A starter home in a higher-priced market may thus have some combination of better-grade kitchen cabinets and countertops, more expensive appliances and carpets, and more finished carpentry around doors and windows than one located in a lower-priced market.

MEASURING LOCAL MARKET COMPETITION

Given that housing costs can vary substantially from one part of the country to another, the performance of an individual builder reflects not only operational efficiency, but also local housing market conditions. In metropolitan areas where there is strong population growth, where buildable land is generally available, and where a competitive home building sector can respond quickly to changing demand, larger companies should see advantages from their size. For example, through their ability to invest in preassembly facilities or better IT systems, larger builders should achieve greater efficiency at the construction site as well as save on materials costs.

In markets where land use restrictions or other factors limit the amount of entitled land, however, efficient operations matter less to profitability. In these circumstances, though, size of operations can be a plus in that only larger, better financed builders may have the resources to guide a parcel of land through the time-consuming and expensive entitlement process. Indeed, home building in these markets is often concentrated in the hands of a few larger builders. With development requiring longer lead times, the supply of new homes cannot respond as quickly to increases in demand, often resulting in more upward pressure on house prices.

Since housing market competitiveness is difficult to measure directly, the Harvard Home Builder Study investigated the use of three proxies for this concept, each touching on a different aspect of local competition: house price appreciation, builder concentration, and estimated time to entitle land.

Home price appreciation at the metropolitan area level was measured using the Office of Federal Housing Enterprise Oversight (OFHEO) House Price Index.[1] In contrast to sales prices for existing homes collected by the National Association of Realtors®, or for new homes collected by the US Census Bureau, the OFHEO House Price Index is based on repeat sales, meaning that it measures average price

---

1   OFHEO was incorporated into the newly created Federal Housing Finance Agency (FHFA) when President Bush signed the Housing and Economic Recovery Act of 2008 into law.

changes in repeat sales or refinancing of the same properties.[2] As such, this index distinguishes changes in home prices from changes in the characteristics of homes sold (e.g., more luxury homes may be sold during one period, and more entry-level homes during another).

A clear advantage to using house price appreciation data to estimate market competitiveness is that it is available for all major US metropolitan areas. Among the 25 metros where divisional respondents to the Harvard Home Builder Survey operated, house price appreciation from 1999 to 2004 ranged from less than 20 percent in Salt Lake City to almost 115 percent in Riverside **(Figure 2.1)**. The average increase was just over 50 percent.

FIGURE 2.1

House Price Appreciation Ranged Widely Across the Metros Covered in the Study

Increase in house prices in 1999–2004 (percent)

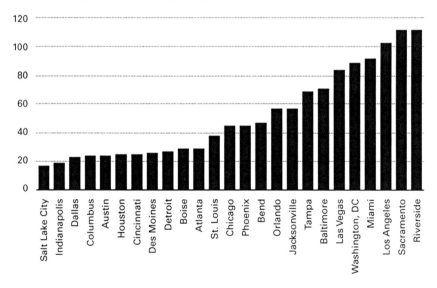

Source: Office of Federal Housing Enterprise Oversight, 2004:4 House Price Index.

The second proxy—builder concentration measured as the aggregate share of new home construction captured by the top five builders in a given metro area—would seem to be a direct measure of local competitiveness since greater concentration implies that fewer major builders are competing in the market. However, the available data did not show much variation in the builder sample. Of the metro areas covered in this study, the top five builders within each metro controlled between 20 percent

---

2   This information is obtained by reviewing repeat mortgage transactions for single-family properties whose mortgages have been purchased or securitized by Fannie Mae or Freddie Mac since January 1975.

and 40 percent of the market in 2004 in all but seven cases—a fairly narrow band given the significant observed differences in financial and operational performance by these divisions.[3]

The final proxy for local market competitiveness tested for this study is the time required for the land entitlement process. Builder divisions in metropolitan areas with longer entitlement times would be less able to adjust construction levels to changing demand for new housing. In addition, markets with longer times to entitle would likely have less competition because fewer builders would have the resources to either hold the land for extended periods or pay more for land that has already been shepherded through the entitlement process.

However, respondents to the Harvard Home Builder Survey indicated that time to entitle land varied significantly even within the same metropolitan area **(Figure 2.2)**. For example, the six survey participants in Sacramento reported entitlement times from 12 months to 36 months. Answers from three respondents in Chicago ranged from 15 months to 36 months, while those from two respondents in Austin ranged from 6 months to 36 months. These broad ranges suggest that either different jurisdictions within each metro area took different amounts of time to handle the entitlement process, or the entitlement process was streamlined in cases where the local jurisdiction saw public benefit from the development. Because of the wide variation reported, developing an accurate metro-wide estimate of time to entitle was problematic.

3   Builder concentration is measured as the percentage of new homes built in a metro area by the largest five local builders, based on the Hanley Wood Market Intelligence 2004 Local Leaders list published in *Builder* magazine.

FIGURE 2.2

Time to Entitle Land Also Varied Greatly Across Metro Markets

Average number of months required to subdivide and entitle land in 2004

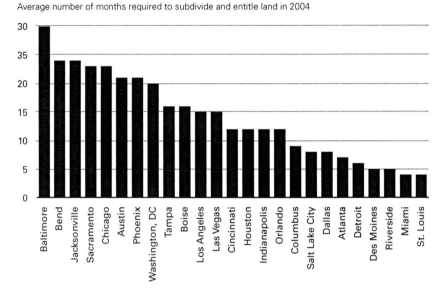

Note: Estimates are the average of responses for builder divisions serving particular markets.
Source: Harvard Home Builder Study, Division Survey, 2005.

Of the three proxies for housing market competitiveness, house price appreciation proved to be the most useful measure. In lower-appreciation markets, housing supply apparently meets or exceeds market demand. In higher-appreciation markets, demand exceeds restricted supply, thereby driving up prevailing prices. This makes these markets attractive to builders that have access to them (i.e., an ability to entitle land).

Given the localized nature of many aspects of home building—zoning laws, availability of land for new construction, supply of capable contractors, and access to skilled and unskilled workers—one would expect that local market conditions affect the operational performance of large-scale home builders. As later chapters demonstrate, looking at the intersection of local conditions (particularly price appreciation) with size of home builders provides the clearest insight into what was—and was not—happening in the realm of on-site operations.[4]

---

4   For the analysis of the survey data, lower house price appreciation markets were defined as those metropolitan areas with less than a 60 percent increase in prices from 1999 to 2004 (as calculated by the OFHEO House Price Index), and higher-appreciation markets had an increase in house prices of 60 percent or more. The breakpoint of 60 percent was chosen because it was the average appreciation of the 62 builder divisions operating in identified metro areas. This definition resulted in 37 builder divisions (about 60 percent) classified as operating in lower-appreciation markets and 25 divisions in higher-appreciations markets. While changing the breakpoint of lower- and higher-appreciation markets to the median appreciation for the divisions or for the 25 metros represented in the survey (46 percent in either case) would have resulted in a more even split of the divisions (with 32 operating in lower-appreciation markets and 30 in higher-appreciation markets), it did not significantly affect any outcomes of the analysis.

SURVEY COVERAGE AND CONTENT

A total of 22 of the nation's 34 largest home builders participated in the Harvard Home Builder Survey. With minimum sales of 2,500 units per year, these 22 companies accounted for almost three-quarters of the homes closed by large builders (selling at least 500 units) in 2004. Of the sample of 44 smaller builders that closed 500–2,499 homes in that year, 19 completed the survey. Overall, survey respondents closed more than 60 percent of the homes sold by companies producing at least 500 homes in 2004 **(Figure 2.3)**.

FIGURE 2.3

Survey Respondents Accounted for More than 60 Percent of Homes Sold by Larger Builders in 2004

Builder Size (By number of homes sold in 2004)	Total Number of Builders	Sample Size	Number of Respondents	Response Rate (Percent)	Share of Total Closings (Percent)
10,000 and Over	10	10	8	80.0	77.4
2,500–9,999	24	24	14	58.3	69.8
1,000–2,499	46	22	8	36.4	18.2
500–999	61	22	11	50.0	16.7
All (500+)	141	78	41	52.6	61.2

Sources: Harvard Home Builder Study, Corporate Survey, 2005; *Builder* magazine's 2004 "Builder 100" list.

In total, the 41 participating home builders completed 88 divisional surveys. Builders selling at least 10,000 homes a year had operations in most if not all of the five regions used for this study. Even smaller builders often served multiple regions and therefore reported for multiple divisions **(Figure 2.4)**.

FIGURE 2.4

Multiple Divisions of Home Builder Companies Participated in the Study

Builder Size (By number of homes sold in 2004)	Number of Builders Reporting	Number of Divisions Reporting	Avg. No. of Divisions Reporting per Builder
10,000 and Over	8	35	4.4
2,500–9,999	14	27	1.9
1,000–2,499	8	13	1.6
500–999	11	13	1.2
All (500+)	41	88	2.1

Source: Harvard Home Builder Study, Corporate and Division Surveys, 2005.

Since home building practices can vary considerably across different parts of the country, the inclusion of builder divisions helped ensure coverage that reflected this diversity. Three-quarters of the divisional offices were located in the more rapidly growing Southeast, Southwest, and Western regions **(Figure 2.5)**. Most of these divisional offices operated in one of 25 identified metropolitan areas, ensuring that differences in local market conditions could be included as part of this research.

FIGURE 2.5

Sunbelt Markets Are Heavily Represented in the Sample
Region served by division (percent of total)

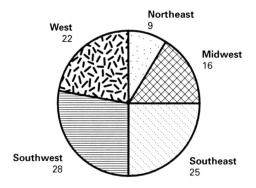

Notes: The Northeast region includes CT, DE, ME, MD, MA, NH, NJ, NY, PA, RI, VA, VT, Wash. DC, and WV. The Midwest includes IA, ID, IN, IL, KS, KY, MI, MN, MT, MO, NE, ND, OH, SD, WI, and WY. The Southeast includes AL, AR, FL, GA, LA, MS, NC, SC, and TN. The Southwest includes AZ, CO, NM, OK, TX, and UT. The West includes AK, CA, HI, NV, OR, and WA.
Source: Harvard Home Builder Study, Division Survey, 2005.

STRUCTURE OF THE SURVEY
The Harvard Home Builder Study attempted to reveal how home building might evolve in light of the experience of other industries that had undergone consolidation. Drawing on these insights, the "virtuous circle" research hypothesis described in Chapter 1 (see **Figure 1.5**) predicts that consolidation provides large home builders with the incentive and the resources to implement operational practices that would help them outperform their smaller competitors.

To test this overarching hypothesis, the research team developed a comprehensive questionnaire asking builders to document their operations in one of the most extensive surveys of large builder activities in the United States.[5] Given that a corporate parent can leverage different scale economies than a single builder division, the

---

5   The survey instruments used for collecting data are available online through the Joint Center for Housing Studies (www.jchs.harvard.edu) and at the Harvard Center for Textile and Apparel Research (www.hctar.org).

survey was broken into two parts—one questionnaire for corporate-level respondents and one for division-level respondents.

The size of corporate operations, measured in homes sold per year, influences access to capital markets and therefore the ability to secure relatively stable low-cost financing. In addition, corporate size generally determines the purchasing power a company can wield in negotiating with national suppliers for preferred pricing and services. Finally, corporate size helps to determine the extent of resources that can be invested in IT systems to manage local operations and ensure standardized procedures across divisions. The corporate-level questionnaire therefore investigated the following areas of activity:

1. **Financial performance,** including growth in the company from 1999 to 2004; types of functions performed by corporate staff; land acquisition strategies; key financial measures (e.g., cost of capital, net income); and other performance measures (e.g., production cycle time, gross margins, and average construction cost per square foot).

2. **Supply chain management,** including general strategy for interacting and communicating with suppliers; number of suppliers for key product lines; corporate negotiated pricing procedures; and detailed procurement procedures for four basic product lines (OSB/plywood/sheathing, wallboard, siding, and windows).

3. **Information technology,** including use of IT systems for estimating, bidding, scheduling, presentations, and communications with homebuyers.

In contrast to overall corporate size, the size of divisional operations generally influences on-site organization—including coordination of labor, scheduling, and pre-assembly—as well as the purchasing power a builder can use to negotiate with local and regional suppliers. Builder divisions frequently make product decisions, both because consumer preferences vary from market to market and because many commodities such as drywall, cement, and dimensional lumber are often locally sourced. Moreover, subcontracting and construction management decisions are typically made at the division level, which also influences product choices because subcontractors frequently purchase products for installation.

Survey participants were asked to identify the regions of the country where they operated. For each of up to five regions, they designated at least one office to complete the divisional survey covering the activities that would likely be managed at the local level. The divisional questionnaire focused on the following areas:

1. **Operational and financial performance,** including growth in size between 1999 and 2004; types of homes constructed and typical sales prices for each of these types; land acquisition strategies; distribution of building costs for labor and materials; overall financial measures; performance in key segments served (e.g. entry-level, tradeup); and product offerings in homes.

2. **Labor and subcontracting,** including size of on-site construction staff; number of subcontracting firms used; direct construction costs by building phase; number of days required for key construction phases; method of awarding work to contractors; and insurance and training offered to subcontractors.

3. **Supply chain management,** including types of suppliers for specific product lines (OSB/plywood/sheathing, wallboard, siding, and windows); services offered by each type of supplier; principal decisionmaker (subcontractor, builder, or homebuyer) in specifying key product lines; preassembly/installation services offered by suppliers by component; and extent of direct negotiations with manufacturers on pricing and services for key product lines.

4. **Information and communication technology,** including areas of the operation that were computerized; communications with subcontractors on scheduling; extent to which information on planned building activity was shared with suppliers and subcontractors; and information sharing with homebuyers on construction status.

An industry advisory committee comprising senior company officials on the Policy Advisory Board of Harvard's Joint Center for Housing Studies helped to design the questionnaire and reviewed early drafts (see Appendix A for a list of members). Several members of the committee offered to pretest the questionnaires at their companies before the final survey was launched. Abt Associates, a professional survey research firm, carried out the online survey effort and provided telephone followup as required to answer questions.

3

BIG BUILDERS AT THE CORPORATE LEVEL

As a result of their rapid consolidation in the 1990s, large-scale home builders took on new or expanded functions in the areas of accessing capital, land assembly, and branding. Given the unusually strong housing market conditions at the time, controlling desirable land positions and efficiently guiding properties through the entitlement process often provided a formula for success. Many larger builders also recognized the critical importance of creating a consistent, positive customer experience as a way to support their expansion. The common denominator for all these activities is that they had to be addressed at the corporate level.

This chapter presents results from the corporate portion of the Harvard Home Builder Survey. After a review of overall performance in 1999–2004, the next section explores what large builders considered the sources of their financial success. The chapter then focuses on how big home builders tackled three key business functions: securing capital for land acquisition and expansion; undertaking land assembly and development; and building a distinctive brand in the minds of consumers. This discussion provides an important context for understanding how and where builders used their growing scale to improve performance.

BUILDER PERFORMANCE DURING THE BOOM

Large home builders saw their profits soar during the housing market boom. Respondents to the Harvard Home Builder Survey reported that gross margins on homes (the markup of the builder's cost) jumped almost four percentage points on average between 1999 and 2004 **(Figure 3.1)**. Their net income before taxes also increased a full three percentage points from 8 percent to 11 percent.

FIGURE 3.1

Large Builder Performance Improved Markedly During the Boom Years

Median for builders providing responses for both years

	1999	2004
Gross Margins (percent)	20.0	23.9
Net Income (percent of revenue)	8	11
Customer Satisfaction (percent willing to recommend)	82	90
Number of Homes Sold	1,713	3,419
Share of Homes Presold (percent)	75	80

Note: Presold homes are defined as having a signed purchase agreement in place before construction began.
Source: Harvard Home Builder Study, Corporate Survey, 2005.

In addition to revenue growth, big builders' performance along other dimensions improved as well. For example, survey participants were able to boost their customer satisfaction ratings from 82 percent to 90 percent on average. The scale of local operations also increased, with the average number of homes sold doubling from 1,713 units to 3,419 units. At the same time, large builders also reported increasing the share of presold homes from 75 percent to 80 percent over the period, reducing their exposure to demand-side risk.

Few respondents to the Harvard Home Builder Survey attributed their performance to more efficient operations as measured by lower construction cycle time and savings on product purchases or other supply chain enhancements. Instead, more than half of the home builders surveyed pointed to the importance of strong market conditions, while more than 30 percent attributed their success to their land assembly strategy **(Figure 3.2)**. Another 13 percent identified improved customer satisfaction as critical.

FIGURE 3.2

A Majority of Large Builders Attributed Their Success to Improved Market Conditions

Percent of builders rating factors most important to profitability in 1999–2004

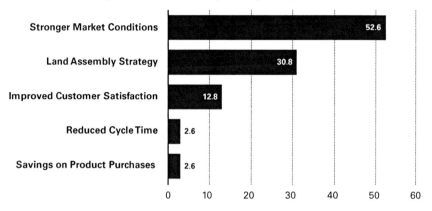

Source: Harvard Home Builder Study, Corporate Survey, 2005.

Moreover, there was often no direct connection between builder size and operating performance. Construction costs per square foot, a key measure of operational performance, showed only modest differences by size of builder operations. In those cases where the disparity is more sizable—such as levels of customer satisfaction and construction cycle time—builders selling fewer homes in fact outperformed the larger firms (Figure 3.3).

FIGURE 3.3

Larger Builders Did Not Outperform Their Smaller Competitors on Key Operational Measures

Median values by builder size

	Number of Homes Sold in 2004		
	Under 2,500	2,500–9,999	10,000 and Over
Cycle Time (days)	110.0	132.5	140.0
Construction Costs per Sq. Ft. (dollars)	50	53	52
Customer Satisfaction (percent willing to recommend)	90.0	92.0	85.5

Source: Harvard Home Builder Study, Corporate Survey, 2005.

The absence of large differences in builder performance by corporate size, and the fact that the differences that did exist were opposite of those expected, is puzzling. One possible explanation lies in the benefits that scale affords with respect to corporate functions that cross local markets, that is, that provide advantages to all divisions of a company. Three corporate-level functions could play this role for home builders. First, a national footprint may be advantageous in securing capital if scale reduces the costs of borrowing or finding investors. Second, scale may provide benefits in creating an apparatus and mechanisms for the costly task of acquiring, entitling, and preparing land for building (particularly in cases where that process is complex and barriers to entry for home builders are high). Finally, scale may allow a national company to take advantage of branding—that is, by creating a distinctive product that consumers are willing to pay a premium to own. The following sections discuss each of these activities in turn.

SECURING CAPITAL FOR EXPANSION

After the implosion of the savings and loan industry in the late 1980s, Wall Street investors helped to fill the financing void for residential developers. Access to capital had become increasingly important as builder operations grew. In addition, companies were looking to expand their land positions in markets where demand for new homes was strong—often locations where it took longer to entitle and prepare land, which increased builders' capital needs.

Bigger home building companies were able not only to secure more capital than their smaller competitors, but also to get better terms because of the perceived stability of their businesses. According to information provided by UBS Investment Bank (2008), larger builders had substantially lower longer-term borrowing costs in 2004 than smaller firms **(Figure 3.4)**. For builders selling 10,000 or more homes a year, the cost of borrowing averaged 160 basis points (1.6 percentage points) below that for builders selling between 2,500 and 9,999 units a year. In addition, many of the largest builders went public over the past few decades, thereby gaining access to equity financing along with borrowed funds. Equity financing is a significant benefit of scale in that it provides companies a steady source of capital during weak as well as strong economic times.[1]

---

1 Most public home builders rely more heavily on equity than debt financing. The survey collected information on the cost of capital, assuming that it would be a more appropriate metric for larger public builders. Given the low borrowing costs in 2004, however, the average reported cost for capital was 10.5 percent, compared with an average of 5.9 percent for loans. For builders of 10,000 homes a year or more, the average cost of capital was 10.2 percent—only slightly better than the average for all builders.

FIGURE 3.4

The Largest Builders Benefited from a More Favorable Cost Structure
Median responses by builder size (percent)

	Number of Homes Sold in 2004			
	Under 2,500	2,500– 9,999	10,000 and Over	All (500+)
Cost of Long-term Debt	N/A	7.8	6.2	7.2
Gross Margin	23.0	24.0	25.1	24.8
EBITDA Margin	13.2	13.5	15.1	14.5
Growth in Homes Sold (1999–2004)	98	79	109	106

Notes: Cost of borrowing long-term debt is as of January 2006 and by number of homes sold in 2008. EBITDA is reported earnings before interest, taxes, depreciation and amortization. Financial information is for public builders only.
Sources: Financial information provided by UBS Investment Bank; growth in homes sold is from the Harvard Home Builder Study, Corporate Survey, 2005.

Lower financing costs were no doubt one reason larger builders significantly outperformed their smaller competitors on key financial indicators. Gross margins among larger firms were 200 basis points better than those of builders selling under 2,500 homes a year, and 100 basis points better than those for builders selling 2,500–9,999 units a year. The advantages of scale showed up most clearly in reported earnings before interest payments, taxes, depreciation, and amortization (EBITDA), where the spread between margins for large builders and their competitors was at least as great as that in gross margins.

Access to capital and the resulting strong earnings provided builders the opportunity to expand their operations. For example, US Commerce Department figures indicate that overall sales of new homes increased just under 37 percent between 1999 and 2004, but home sales more than doubled among the larger builders participating in this study. Indeed, builders closing 10,000 or more homes in 2004 reported the biggest sales gains over this period.

LAND ASSEMBLY STRATEGIES
During the 1980s and 1990s, municipalities turned to a growing list of regulatory actions—including basic zoning, design guidelines, impact fees, environmental regulations, and growth boundaries—to manage or control residential growth. While the precise effect of these regulations on the number of homes built and on home prices differs from one area to another, they generally add time and therefore cost to the construction process. As such, land use regulations limit the number of builders with sufficient resources and capacity to serve particular markets.

According to respondents to the Harvard Home Builder Survey, the time required to entitle land and obtain subdivision permitting varied considerably across metropolitan areas.[2] This process, whereby local officials review proposed projects to ensure compliance with ordinances and design standards, reportedly took as little as four months in some jurisdictions and up to 30 months in others. Five of the top eight areas with the longest entitling times were along the Northeast corridor (Baltimore and Washington, DC) or in the West (Sacramento, Phoenix, and Bend, Oregon). The average time for subdivision and entitlement in these two regions was about 1.5 years, while the average time required to finish land (including site preparation and improvements as well as subdivision and entitlement) totaled two years or more. In the Southeast, in contrast, time to finish land averaged just under 10 months.

Most builders increased their land holdings and expanded land development during the 1999–2004 housing boom because they viewed these activities as key drivers of increased profitability. Owning land outright is the traditional way to control land, although it entails greater risk because it ties up large amounts of capital—particularly when land development patterns in the area change or when the development process becomes more protracted because local regulatory procedures take longer to navigate.

Even as home building firms were growing over this period, they began to leverage their resources to reduce risk by controlling more land through options. Under these contracts, a builder pays the owner for a time-limited right to purchase a parcel in the future at some predetermined price. A report by Moody's Investors Service (2006) notes, however, that there are many types of land options, some of which more closely resemble ownership than others. True options, the report explains, involve a small downpayment (generally under 5 percent), are for raw land, and are a one-off transaction with the landowner, where the builder has no obligation to exercise the option. Options that have ownership characteristics require larger downpayments (typically 15 percent or more), are for fully entitled land with infrastructure, and obligate the builder to exercise the option when performance targets or milestones are reached.

Options arrangements vary across the country. Builders in certain markets—including high demand areas along the West and East Coasts, and particularly in New Jersey—must often put up the full value of the land to secure a position (Bordenaro 2005). In Texas, in contrast, builders can typically pay a 10 percent fee to lock up a land parcel for three to five years.

The importance of these activities is clear from the gross margins that builders in particular parts of the country were able to achieve in 2004. In regions where land use regulations and growth controls were restrictive and housing demand strong, such policies often forced up the price of developable land by limiting its supply or by adding to development costs. Builders that owned land in these areas often profited from the situation and were able to achieve larger gross margins. For example,

---

2   Pendall, Puentes and Martin (2006) also report regional variation in land use regulations. They find that metropolitan areas in the Northeast and Midwest tend to use regulations to exclude most types of growth, while those in the West employ regulations to accommodate and manage growth.

builder divisions in the West, where land regulations are relatively strict, reported average gross margins of 28.4 percent for entry-level homes. In the Northeast, where land restrictions are also common but housing demand was moderate to weak, gross margins averaged 24.2 percent. In other regions, gross margins generally averaged about 20 percent.

With land positions a key ingredient in profitability, builders increasingly focused on this phase of their business in 1999–2004. When asked by the Harvard Home Builder Survey if their land acquisition strategies had changed significantly in recent years, more than three-quarters of division respondents noted an increase in land inventories, while the same share reported an expansion of their land development activities **(Figure 3.5)**. At the same time, builders were also concerned about managing the risk involved in holding land. In 1999–2004, more than half of respondents increased their participation in land-related joint ventures, and more than a third increased their reliance on options and off-balance-sheet arrangements.

FIGURE 3.5

Land Practices Became a Higher Priority During the Housing Boom

Share of divisions reporting how land acquisition strategies changed in recent years (percent)

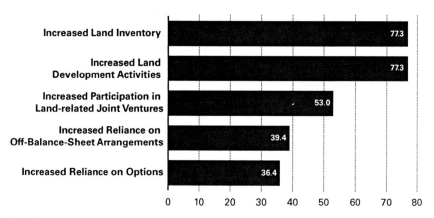

Notes: Estimates are averages across builder divisions. Multiple responses were allowed.
Source: Harvard Home Builder Study, Division Survey, 2005.

By 2004, the average builder in the Harvard Home Builder Study owned enough land to accommodate the next 2.6 years of building at their current rate and had options on land to accommodate another 3.7 years. Builders selling more than 10,000 homes annually both owned and held options on more land relative to their building needs than their smaller counterparts, although the differences were modest. The share of land holdings owned versus optioned was quite similar for builders of all sizes.

While land development activities were often highly profitable for builders, they also added risk. As part of the analysis, the Harvard Home Builder Study developed an "aggressive land practices" variable based on the extent of land holdings and the degree of a builder's participation in additional land development activities. Efforts to reduce risk, such as reliance on off-balance-sheet arrangements, were also factored into the scores.

Larger builders reported more aggressive land practices on average, in part because of their modestly larger holdings, but primarily because of their greater involvement in other land development activities. Individual company scores ranged from 0 to 24, while the average score was 7.7. The scores for builders selling 10,000 or more homes a year averaged two points higher than the average, at 9.7 **(Figure 3.6)**.

FIGURE 3.6

Larger Builders Became More Aggressive in Their Land Practices During the Housing Boom
Averages by corporate size

	Number of Homes Sold in 2004			
	Under 2,500	2,500–9,999	10,000 and Over	All (500+)
Number of Years Land Owned	2.5	2.8	2.8	2.6
Number of Years Land Optioned	3.9	3.3	4.2	3.7
Aggressive Land Practices Score	6.9	7.5	9.7	7.7

Notes: The aggressive land practices score was calculated in the following way. Builders were given one point for each year of land owned at current production levels; one point for each year of land optioned; two points if they increased land development activities in recent years; and two points if they increased their land inventory in recent years. Two points were subtracted if they had increased their reliance on off-balance-sheet arrangements. The highest score for any builder was 24 out of a possible 29.5.
Source: Harvard Home Builder Study, Corporate Survey, 2005.

Local market conditions were also an important factor in land strategies. In markets with lower home price appreciation, builders were somewhat less likely to pursue aggressive land practices. Lower house price appreciation is related to greater availability of land for home building, as well as to more intense market competition. With more land available, builders have less incentive to tie up resources in land positions for long periods of time.

Conversely, markets with higher house price appreciation generally have lower levels of building activity relative to new home demand, often because there is relatively less entitled land. In these markets, builders do have an incentive to increase their land holdings not only because doing so may provide a competitive advantage, but also because entitlement in such areas is likely to be more time-consuming. As a result, builders operating in higher-appreciation markets tended to be slightly more aggressive in their land practices.

While both the size of builder operations and local market characteristics independently influence a firm's land assembly strategy, it is the combination of these factors that makes the greatest difference. Not surprisingly, larger builder divisions located in higher-appreciation markets posted scores that were more than 40 percent above the average for the entire builder sample **(Figure 3.7)**.

FIGURE 3.7

Larger Divisions in Higher-Appreciation Markets Were More Aggressive in Their Land Practices

Average aggressive land practices score

Divisions (By number of homes sold in 2004)	Lower-Appreciation Markets	Higher-Appreciation Markets	All Markets
Smaller (Under 1,000)	6.6	6.6	**6.6**
Larger (1,000 and Over)	7.3	10.0	**8.0**
All Divisions	**6.9**	**7.3**	**7.0**

Notes: Lower-appreciation markets are defined as metro areas with less than a 60% increase in house prices in 1999–2004 (as calculated by the OFHEO House Price Index). House prices in higher-appreciation markets rose 60% or more. Differences are not significant at the 0.05 level.
Source: Harvard Home Builder Study, Division Survey, 2005.

CORPORATE BRANDING AND CUSTOMER SATISFACTION

A distinctive brand enables companies to achieve higher returns by convincing its customers to pay a premium for its products (Keller 2008). A branding strategy attempts to differentiate a product or service from rivals and typically emerges in more concentrated markets. Not surprisingly, as home builders consolidated, they paid greater attention to corporate branding and to creating distinct identities for their product lines. Pulte's Del Webb brand for active adults, Toll Brothers' luxury homes, and Lennar's PowerSmart line of energy-efficient and environmentally friendly houses are but a few examples of efforts to build brand awareness in increasingly competitive markets.

Larger home builders that had grown through acquisitions faced greater challenges because the houses built by acquired companies often had a different look and feel. One way to deal with this issue would have been to keep the prior company's brand and offer it as a complement to current lines supported by the acquiring builder. This strategy would, however, create problems for builders whose long-term goal was to standardize their product offerings across the full range of markets served.

Many analysts viewed national branding as one of the primary potential benefits of home builder consolidation. Indeed, the Andersen Corporate Finance study claimed that "large national builders enjoy significantly enhanced revenues through branding" (DeCain 2002). Companies participating in the Harvard Home Builder Study apparently understood these potential advantages in that they put a great deal of effort and resources into creating brand recognition for and raising customer satisfaction with their products. As Figure 3.2 shows, improving customer satisfaction was ranked third by builders (behind stronger market conditions and land assembly strategy) on the list of factors deemed most important to their recent profitability.

Builders were generally successful in achieving high levels of customer satisfaction. On average in 2004, builders reported that 90 percent of their customers were willing to recommend their firm to friends who might be looking to build new homes. This "willingness to recommend" is considered the gold standard of customer satisfaction. Still, it is somewhat surprising that larger home builders were able to score so high on customer satisfaction given their decentralized structure. Unlike strategies to secure favorable financing or assemble land for development, creating a consistently positive brand image would be a challenge for home builders to achieve on a company-wide basis. As measured by the J.D. Power and Associates New Home Builder Satisfaction Survey, customer satisfaction relates to many policies and practices delivered at the local level.[3] It would thus seem likely that customer satisfaction ratings across a company would vary widely.

The reality was just the opposite. Using publicly available data from J.D. Power's 2006 survey, the research team tested whether major home builders were able to achieve a consistent customer experience across markets. Specifically, the analysis looked at the variation in customer satisfaction both within and across the nation's 10 largest home building companies along four dimensions: overall satisfaction, price and value, quality of workmanship and materials, and home design. For each dimension, customers were asked to rate the company on a scale from 2 (below average) to 5 (among the best).[4] If the variation in scores within a given company was smaller than across different companies, the results would indicate that home builders had indeed achieved consistency.

---

3   The J.D. Power New Home Builder Satisfaction Survey measures satisfaction among buyers of new single-family homes in the nation's largest markets. The survey examines satisfaction with the entire home-buying experience including customer service, sales staff, design center, price/value relationship, design elements, location, recreation and amenities, and quality of workmanship and materials. Homebuyers also provide opinions on their mortgage and title companies, the builder's Web site, and the occurrence and resolution of construction problems. The 2006 survey results were based on 60,927 responses of buyers who had lived in their new homes for 4–18 months.

4   To calculate Power Circle Ratings for home building companies, J.D. Power begins with the overall index scores ranking companies based upon weighted responses to several factors. Using these measurements, Power Circle Ratings are calculated based on the range between the product or service with the highest score and the product or service with the lowest score. The highest-ranking company in each segment receives five Power Circles. In highly competitive segments with many companies, multiple companies scoring in the top 10 percent of all companies in the segment can receive five Power Circles, indicating that consumers rate them "among the best" of all companies in the survey. Companies scoring in the next 30 percent of all companies in the segment receive a rating of 4 Power Circles, indicating that consumers rate them "better than most" among companies in the survey. Companies scoring in the next 30 percent of all companies in the segment receive a rating of 3 Power Circles indicating that consumers rate them "about average" among all companies in the survey. Note that the survey average is established within this score range, with 10 percent of companies rating "about average" receiving a numerical score above the survey average and 20 percent of companies rating "about average" receiving a numerical score below the survey average. Companies or models scoring in the next 30 percent of all companies in the segment receive a rating of 2 Power Circles, indicating that consumers rate them lower than other companies in the survey. For more details, see www.jdpower.com/ratings-guide.

The results suggest that national home builders were successful in this effort. This is apparent in two ways. First, the average scores for each company across the four dimensions of customer satisfaction are unusually consistent (Figure 3.8). For example, of the ten largest home builders, Pulte and Centex always stood at the top of the list along all four dimensions while D.R. Horton and M.D.C. Holdings were always rated at the bottom. The rankings of the other home builders on the list are also remarkably similar across categories, indicating that a home builder's score on one dimension (such as quality) is a good predictor of its score on others.

FIGURE 3.8

Large Home Builders Were Able to Provide a Consistent Customer Experience Across Divisions

J.D. Power customer satisfaction ratings for top 10 home builders, 2006

| Company | Overall Satisfaction | | Quality | | Price | | Design Elements | | Number of Metros |
	Mean	Variance	Mean	Variance	Mean	Variance	Mean	Variance	
Pulte	4.62	0.46	4.59	0.47	4.48	0.47	4.48	0.40	29
Centex	4.52	0.62	4.45	0.61	4.34	0.66	4.38	0.74	29
Lennar	3.38	0.55	3.29	0.51	3.62	0.45	3.10	0.49	21
NVR	3.29	0.57	3.14	0.48	3.00	0.33	3.00	0.33	7
Hovnanian	3.25	0.21	3.13	0.13	3.25	0.21	3.25	0.21	8
KB Home	3.00	0.36	3.04	0.41	3.13	0.30	3.26	0.57	23
Ryland Group	2.76	0.57	2.71	0.60	2.53	0.26	2.76	0.44	17
Beazer	2.67	0.59	2.67	0.71	2.78	0.77	2.83	0.74	18
D.R. Horton	2.28	0.21	2.32	0.23	2.36	0.24	2.24	0.19	25
MDC Holdings/ Richmond American	2.00	0.00	2.00	0.00	2.10	0.10	2.00	0.00	10
Median	3.13	0.5	3.08	0.47	3.07	0.32	3.05	0.42	

Note: The Harvard Home Builder Study did not necessarily include any or all of the top 10 home builders listed here.
Source: Authors' tabulations of the J.D. Power and Associates 2006 New Home Builder Customer Satisfaction Study.

Second, the variation in scores across the 10 companies is much larger than the variation within each company. For example, the difference between the average overall customer satisfaction score for top-rated Pulte (4.62) and the median for all firms (3.13) is about 1.5 points, while the median variance in scores for each company is just 0.5 point. This means that national home builders—despite the inherent difficulties in setting standards for their diverse operations and the unique conditions existing in each market—were somehow able to create a similar experience for buyers across geographic areas.

The costs of creating a common customer experience are considerable. To achieve these results, builders had to standardize their product options, design requirements, building quality, sales protocols, and service procedures, to name but a few of the requisite policies. Clearly, the builders ranking high in customer satisfaction took the challenge of establishing a consistent customer experience as a priority and were successful in creating a positive brand image across multiple customer bases.

CONCLUSION

Given the primary goal of managing rapid growth to achieve financial success, larger home building companies were able to meet key corporate objectives during the 1999–2004 housing boom. In particular, they were able to obtain funding for their expansion plans, and at a cost that was generally below that of their smaller competitors. Big builders were also able to secure long-term financing and thus limit their credit risk. In terms of land assembly, bigger builders were able to acquire large parcels in the most desirable areas through a combination of purchases and options, and had the resources to take these land holdings through the time-consuming entitlement process. Finally, larger home building firms were able to provide a remarkably consistent customer experience across a disparate set of divisional operations. In achieving these objectives, scale played an important role in contributing to builder profitability. Along these dimensions, bigger was indeed better.

While able to make changes requiring little local involvement, large firms found that implementing other company-wide policies—such as training staff to take on expanded responsibilities, introducing new on-site production techniques, adapting longstanding relationships with suppliers and subcontractors, implementing the latest software throughout the company to increase efficiency, using the Internet to coordinate and inform suppliers and subcontractors of job status, and fundamentally changing a corporate culture—was much more challenging.

As such, corporate leaders paid much less attention to areas viewed as making less immediate contributions to profitability, such as improved on-site operations. Given the favorable housing market conditions at the time, home builders' focus on those aspects of business that proved most profitable is understandable—especially in light of the pressure that they were under to generate high rates of return for investors. As the following chapters demonstrate, however, big builders were focused on profitability and therefore were less concerned about making comparable improvements in their on-site operations that could have made a difference in their longer-term financial performance.

4

LABOR AND SUBCONTRACTING PRACTICES

Residential construction entails significant risk management problems. Home builders must secure large tracts of land, entitle them, and prepare them for construction long before carpenters can begin framing and electricians string wires—much less become finished homes that can be sold to generate revenues. Companies must have access to significant pools of capital for acquisitions and tie up substantial amounts of capital in land holdings, material acquisition and building costs.

But construction practices at the work site present another key risk. In essence, the longer it takes to turn a vacant parcel of land into a finished home that can lead to a financial transaction with a buyer, the greater the cost and risk to the builder. At the same time, home builders must balance efforts to shorten construction cycle time against the direct costs of construction. Direct costs may be reduced by building multiple houses simultaneously, coordinating work crews, and making sure that the overall management of subcontractors leads to efficient scheduling and construction.

Drawing on results from the Harvard Home Builder Survey, this chapter looks at how home builders managed construction during the housing boom, including their use of subcontractors, bidding of work, and adoption of other coordination methods. The analysis relates builders' ability to coordinate on-site production with construction costs and the amount of time required to perform specific activities. Where possible, the discussion tests the predictions of the virtuous circle hypothesis and examines differences in outcomes across higher- and lower-appreciation markets.

Regardless of scale or market type, home builders in the survey relied on a construction manager (CM) model of production, coordinating the activities of a large number of basic construction and specialty trade subcontractors but directly employing few workers. This has historically been the large home builder's role and is unlikely to change in the future for a variety of reasons. The survey evidence does suggest, however, that builders have not capitalized significantly on their growing scale to perform their construction management role more efficiently. In fact, across a wide variety of practices at the division level, the largest home builders were no more likely, and in some cases less likely, to adopt advanced coordination and construction practices than smaller builders in the sample. As a result, performance—as measured in terms of costs and cycle times for construction—did not improve with builder size.

At the same time, the evidence indicates that the *type* of market in which a home builder operated had a significant impact on on-site practices and performance. In particular, firms operating in markets where price appreciation was relatively low between 1999 and 2004 made greater efforts to improve coordination at the job site than those operating in markets where price appreciation was relatively high. Similarly, builders in lower-appreciation markets had lower costs and shorter cycle times than comparable builders in higher-appreciation markets.

The findings in this chapter underscore the tensions that national home builders face by distancing themselves from on-site construction activities. While the construction management model shields home builders from many day-to-day coordination problems, it also prevents them from capturing many of the potential benefits of scale—including better coordination of contractors and subcontractors, improved performance arising from long-term relationships with the workforce, and diffusion of best practices. In the coming recovery, home builders must reconsider the hands-off approach that they have traditionally taken to coordination at the construction site.

THE CONSTRUCTION MANAGER MODEL

A construction project of any complexity requires coordinating large numbers of separate business enterprises and workers with varied responsibilities, skills, and roles. In other sectors of the industry such as commercial or public construction, a general contractor (GC) traditionally filled the role of coordinator, managing the project and directly hiring workers in the basic trades. Having a lead contractor goes back to the early days of modern industry, when a mason contractor typically played this central role.[1] Like the mason builder at the turn of the 20th century, the GC was also responsible for overseeing and coordinating the work of subcontractors in skilled and semiskilled trades such as electrical, plumbing, sheet metal, and roofing (Dunlop 1961 and 1993, Weil 2005).

Since the early 1980s, however, a different type of project manager has replaced the GC in commercial and industrial construction. The construction manager or CM works for the owner/developer and coordinates with architects and engineers. Unlike a GC, a construction manager does not directly employ any workers on the site. Instead, the CM hires contractors in the basic trades as well as specialty trades. This removes the CM from many of the responsibilities of employing workers.

---

1   John R. Commons, a labor economist of that era, noted: "The mason builder, or general contractor, secures the contract from the owner, or 'client,' and generally puts up the brick-work; but he sublets, by competitive bidding, all of the other work to as many contractors as there are kinds of work. This system enables the contractor to enter the field with little or no capital, since it is usually arranged that partial payments shall be made by the owner to the general contractor, and by him to the sub-contractors, as the work progresses" (Commons 1904, p. 410).

Given that their compensation depends on overall performance at the work site, construction managers bear some of the risk arising from the vagaries of construction. But because they employ only a small percentage of the workforce, CMs can shift much of the risk onto subcontractors when unexpected conditions occur. This has increased the cost pressures on the group of firms now acting in the construction roles formerly held by GCs, as well as on other subcontractors involved in the project.

Since their emergence after World War II, large home builders have served as developers of land parcels as well as overseers of the construction process. Even when much of the construction industry relied on GCs to play the pivotal role of lead contractor, residential construction drew on the CM model.[2] The long embrace on this management model has had major implications for how builders have taken advantage of their increasing scale.

Some 90 percent of respondents to the Harvard Home Builder Survey reported that they held primary responsibility for coordinating labor; in only a very small share of cases did a general contractor (5 percent) or separate developer (4 percent) play this role. Yet they discharged this responsibility by coordinating other contractors rather than by directly employing workers on the job site. This strategy is apparent from the fact that payments to subcontractors made up builders' largest cost category, representing almost 40 percent of all major expenses **(Figure 4.1)**.[3] In contrast, expenses for on-site labor (workers directly employed by the home builders for construction) accounted for less than 5 percent of all major expenses. Reliance on subcontractors did not vary much with corporate or division size from 1999 to 2004, with larger-scale builders devoting about the same share of expenses to on-site labor as smaller builders.

---

2   Even the famed Levittown housing project, an early example of a large-scale subdivision that was designed, managed, and built by the Levitt family in the late 1940s, used a subcontracting model for construction. However, William Levitt tightly managed the activities of these contractors.

3   This estimate is lower than that reported in a study by the National Association of Home Builders. Using Census of Construction data, Ahluwalia (2003) reported that about 60 percent of on-site costs arise from work subcontracted out to others among "operative builders," i.e., the census category that includes all of the home builders in the sample. However, this calculation excludes permitting costs, equipment rental, and other corporate overhead costs that make up the total expenses cited here.

FIGURE 4.1

Payments to Subcontractors Are By Far the Largest Expense for Home Builders

Average share of expenses in 2004 (percent)

Payments to Subcontractors (Including cost of materials purchased directly)	38.5
Land Purchases	15.7
Product and Material Purchases	12.4
Land Development/Entitlement/Preparation	8.8
Sales and Marketing	7.8
Corporate Overhead	6.3
On-site Payroll Employees	4.2
Financing	3.4
Other	2.2

Source: Harvard Home Builder Study, Division Survey, 2005.

The typical respondent to the Harvard Home Builder Survey closed on 6,900 homes in 2004, with some of the largest companies posting sales of well over 10,000 units. But even at that scale, these major home builders employed a very small workforce. The largest number of employees directly hired by contractors was in the category of construction managers/superintendents, with an average of 48 people employed per division **(Figure 4.2)**. In contrast, builders hired a trivial number of carpenters, electricians, plumbers, or other crafts, with none exceeding 10 employees. Once again, the low number of directly employed workers differed little between smaller and larger firms in the survey sample.

FIGURE 4.2

Although Adding Employees During the Boom, Major Home Builders Still Kept a Cap on Payrolls

Average number of employees by division

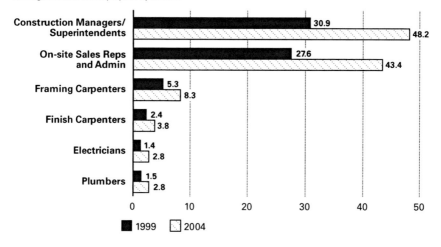

Source: Harvard Home Builder Study, Division Survey, 2005.

Moreover, reliance on outside subcontractors for on-site construction work did not change during the housing boom. The number of workers directly hired for these activities increased only modestly between 1999 and 2004, even though the average number of homes built per division jumped almost 60 percent from 733 to 1,158.

Not surprisingly, home builders rely extensively on subcontractors. Carpenters and helpers involved in framing constitute the largest group in terms of construction costs and number of contractors used **(Figure 4.3)**. In 2004, home builder divisions used an average of 10 framing carpenter subcontractors for completing work on projects. They also drew on large numbers of finish carpenters and bricklayers/masons/tile setters, but a smaller number of subcontractors for completing electrical or plumbing work. Survey respondents reported an increase in their use of all types of subcontractors during the housing market boom. For example, the average number of carpenters (framing and finish combined) rose from about 12 in 1999 to 16 in 2004.[4]

---

4   Ahluwalia (2003) shows similar reliance in the use of subcontractors for a wide variety of services, as well as growth in reliance on subcontractors in virtually all types of residential construction jobs between 1994 and 2002.

FIGURE 4.3

The Use of Subcontractors Also Increased During the Boom

Average number of subcontracting firms hired by builder divisions

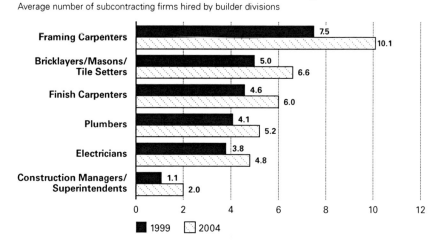

Note: Observations are matched across years within category.
Source: Harvard Home Builder Study, Division Survey, 2005.

However, growth in overall building activity far outstripped increases in the average number of subcontracting firms used by these builders. In 1999, the average home builder in the sample sold about 121 homes per framing contractor hired. By 2004, that number increased to 169 homes. Similarly large increases in homes sold relative to subcontractors hired were also found among other construction crafts **(Figure 4.4)**. In most cases, home builders reported relying on their top three subcontractors for 20 percent of subcontracting in a specific trade. The share of work supplied by top subcontractors changed little between 1999 and 2004, suggesting that home builders were giving more work to their subcontractor pools rather than concentrating the increased work among a small number of major subcontractors.

FIGURE 4.4

Builder Divisions Dramatically Increased Sales of Homes per Subcontracting Firm by 2004

Average number of houses sold per subcontracting firm

	1999	2004	Percent Change
Framing Carpenters	121	169	39.7
Finish Carpenters	145	203	40.0
Electricians	162	238	46.9
Plumbers	160	227	41.9
Bricklayers/Masons/Tile Setters	132	186	40.9

Note: Averages were calculated by dividing total number of houses sold by total number of subcontracting firms hired to perform each type of craft for each division, and then finding the average ratio among the divisions.
Source: Harvard Home Builder Study, Division Survey, 2005.

If the growing scale of a home builder division increased the number of homes built per contractor, larger companies would presumably be able to build homes of a given quality with less labor input than smaller firms. The reliance on subcontractors, however, makes this type of comparison impossible. Nevertheless, comparing the number of homes sold per construction manager for a division provides a rough gauge of the efficiency of home builders of different sizes and operating in higher- and lower-appreciation markets.

Regardless of market type, larger home builders did in fact sell more homes per construction manager than smaller home builders (Figure 4.5). This relationship also exists in both lower- and higher-appreciation markets. For example, small divisions operating in higher-appreciation markets in 2004 sold 7 homes per construction manager while large divisions sold 32. There are similar, though smaller, scale effects in lower-appreciation markets. The ratio of homes sold per construction manager between 1999 and 2004 remained relatively constant in both lower- and higher-appreciation markets overall. Although only a rough approximation of productivity, this measure provides evidence that scale may have conferred some production benefits to larger home builders during the boom.

FIGURE 4.5

Larger Builders Outstripped Smaller Competitors in Some Measures of Efficiency

Median number of homes sold per construction manager

Divisions (By number of homes sold in 2004)	Lower-Appreciation Markets		Higher-Appreciation Markets		All Markets	
	1999	2004	1999	2004	1999	2004
Small (Under 500)	23	15	19	7	20	13
Medium (500–999)	19	21	20	19	19	21
Large (1,000 and over)	26	28	23	32	25	30
All	24	24	20	17	21	22

Notes: Observations are matched across years. The differences between small and large home builders are not statistically significant except for builders in higher-appreciation markets in 2004 (0.05 level).
Source: Harvard Home Builder Study, Division Survey, 2005.

BENEFITS AND COSTS OF IMPROVED COORDINATION

From a risk management perspective, home builders enjoy clear benefits from rely-ing primarily on subcontractors for construction. By keeping the labor force at arm's length, home builders are shielded from the inevitable ups and downs of the con-struction market and the consequent need to lay off workers or keep them on the rolls during the business cycle.[5] Home builders also avoid many of the quasi-fixed costs associated with employment, ranging from those involved in screening and hiring workers to payment of certain social costs (such as workers compensation and unemployment insurance) and other benefits that do not vary directly with hours worked. This type of relationship with the labor force also reduces builders' exposure to potentially large liabilities arising from workplace accidents.

But the construction manager model also entails significant costs and risks that may be less apparent. First, the CM model requires that home builders create incentives via market- rather than organization-based relationships (see Eccles 1981). In some cases, this may be advantageous. For example, if significant numbers of subcon-tractors are available to undertake a given activity, the bidding process can put downward pressure on the costs for different crafts. Similarly, they can put pressure on contractors to compete on the amount of time required for completing work (which is linked to the direct costs of contracting via productivity and to the time-to-completion for the larger project).

---

5   The exception is the large number of workers employed directly in sales, marketing, and construction management. Not surprisingly, the recent downturn in the housing market has been accompanied by signifi-cant employment cutbacks in these categories as well.

At the same time, reliance on subcontracting and market relationships can have a downside. In particular, if the pool of contractors is constrained, the bidding process may lead to rapidly escalating prices for key skills, especially in high-growth markets. Depending on ease of entry of new workers into the trades, these might be significant drivers of cost. Difficulties can also arise from problems monitoring the performance of subcontractors, misalignment between the incentives of home builders and subcontractors, or both.

Moreover, the CM model may hinder larger home builders from taking full advantage of scale economies arising at the division level. The ability to construct hundreds or even thousands of homes in a major development may present opportunities for dramatically changing on-site practices, such as adopting the most efficient construction practices across sites to improve productivity and sequencing the phases of building to reduce wait time and delays.[6] But this requires more direct involvement with project management than the CM model typically provides.

The complexities of managing multiple sites also present challenges. As noted previously, major home builders increased their capacity to manage risk during the housing boom by cutting back on speculative building. Recall that major builders had reduced the share of speculative homes to 33 percent in 2004, down from 36 percent in 1999.[7] Gearing construction more closely to market conditions requires shorter cycles between the time a buyer commits to a home and when the home is completed. This, in turn, implies greater ability to coordinate work on the job site.

A final set of problems posed by the CM model relates more to public policy than to home builder performance per se. By removing itself from the direct employer role and drawing on highly competitive markets for contracting and subcontracting, the CM model can lead to poor working conditions. This is particularly true when large pools of workers are seeking jobs, large numbers of small contractors are acting as intermediaries, and the prices received by those contractors are under pressure. Since labor represents the single largest cost for most subcontractors, the incentives to cut such costs in any way possible are high. The widespread use of undocumented workers from Mexico as well as Central and South America further contributes to the downward pressures on wages and erosion of working conditions.

A recent study of labor standards violations among low-wage workers in three major metropolitan areas bears this out (Bernhardt et al. 2009). The researchers found that

---

6   William Levitt applied the mass-production assembly line model to home building, allowing him to move workers from site to site. Hale (2009) notes, "*Life, Newsweek, Time,* and many other magazines delighted in the story of the painter whose sole job was to paint the window sills of each house; but the example was an apt one, for by moving crews of workers sequentially from house to house, Levitt avoided the necessity of craft workers, unions, and the rest. In addition, his program could tolerate high labor turnover, a dreaded feature of the new prosperity after the end of the war. If one worker left, another could be quickly hired and trained as a replacement."

7   Homebuyers did, however, have a number of ways to get out of a "presold" agreement. Although this may have meant losing a deposit of several thousand dollars, purchasers in many high-appreciation markets were able to get out of agreements for substantially less (and sometimes nothing) given the ample supply of new buyers. The percentage of homes built on a speculative basis was therefore higher than these figures suggest.

12.7 percent of residential construction workers surveyed had experienced minimum wage violations. More striking, about 70.5 percent of those workers were not paid overtime in violation of federal and state laws, and 72.2 percent were subject to "off-the-clock" violations—that is, nonpayment for work for which they were entitled to compensation. This pattern of violations is not unusual where the employment relationship has been fissured away from larger employers to numerous small employers through contracting and subcontracting (Weil 2010).

COORDINATING ON-SITE ACTIVITIES

How large home builders coordinate site-level activities provides several opportunities to enhance the benefits and mitigate the costs of the construction management model. Coordination involves such practices as bidding new work, allying with select subcontractors, and taking advantage of information technology to manage activities of contractors at the work site.

Awarding work to subcontractors. The methods that home builders use to select contractors can have a significant impact on their ability to coordinate activities once construction begins. Hands-off market-based relationships where new work is openly bid to a wide field of potential contractors may help home builders reduce the prices that subcontractors offer. But purely market-based relationships may also leave home builders with contractors that are unable to build to the quality specified or to coordinate well with the home builder or other contractors. These concerns may encourage builders to bid work to a smaller group of well-regarded subcontractors or to have even closer associations with a smaller set of key companies.

Although bidding practices are similar across firms of different sizes, the evidence from the Harvard Home Builder Survey indicates that builders award work differently depending on where they operate.[8] Competitive bidding among a restricted set of subcontractors is the most common type of arrangement for awarding work to carpenters and electrical and plumbing contractors **(Figure 4.6)**. This system potentially combines the benefits of competitive bidding (downward price pressure) with those of having affiliated subcontractors (better coordination and quality control as well as higher experience levels). Home builders rely on this hybrid form of bidding particularly for highly skilled trades such as plumbing and electrical work. Indeed, firms operating in lower-appreciation markets in 1999–2004 awarded about half of all carpentry work and close to two-thirds of plumbing and electrical work via restricted bids.

---

8   Figure 4.6 excludes a fourth category of awarding work, "using captive subcontractors" (where builders hold an equity stake in the companies) because of the tiny number of respondents using this type of arrangement.

FIGURE 4.6

Market Characteristics Influence How Home Builders Award Specialty Trade Work to Subcontractors

Share of home builder divisions (percent)

	Lower-Appreciation Markets			Higher-Appreciation Markets		
	Open Competitive Bid	Restricted Bid	Affiliated Subs	Open Competitive Bid	Restricted Bid	Affiliated Subs
Framing Carpenters	22	47	31	9	87	4
Finish Carpenters	21	48	30	13	83	4
Electricians	21	64	15	4	91	4
Plumbers	21	64	15	4	91	4

Notes: "Open competitive bid" allows bidding among all interested subcontractors; "restricted bid" limits bidding to a group of contractors specified by the home builder; "affiliated subs" awards work to independent subcontractors affiliated in some way with the home builder. Only a tiny number of builders awarded work to a fourth category of captive subcontractors, or companies where the builders hold an equity stake. Differences between lower- and higher-appreciation markets are statistically significant at a 0.05 level for framing and finishing carpenters and at a 0.10 level for electricians and plumbers.
Source: Harvard Home Builder Study, Division Survey, 2005.

Bidding practices were strikingly different in lower- and higher-appreciation markets. Home builders in lower-appreciation areas used open competitive bidding to a far greater extent. About 21 percent of contracts were awarded to plumbers and electricians on this basis, compared with only 4 percent in higher-appreciation markets. Similarly, builders in lower-appreciation markets seemed to award work to affiliated subcontractors much more frequently. This implies that in markets where home builders were under greater pressure to reduce costs, firms tended to use a wider assortment of practices—whether open competitive bidding or using affiliated subcontractors—than the hybrid form of bidding used almost exclusively by builders in higher-appreciation markets.

Consolidating the subcontractor base. In the 1990s major retailers like Walmart, manufacturers like Toyota, and service companies like Marriott experienced rapid growth in the number of suppliers. Many of these companies responded by consolidating their supplier base to improve quality and efficiency and to reduce the complexity of coordination.

Large home builders face a similar challenge in relying on multiple contractors and subcontractors. Builders can balance their objectives of holding down subcontracting costs and efficiently coordinating multiple activities by concentrating their work among a smaller number of subcontractors. By doing so, builders can draw on a proven set of companies. On the one hand, this may strengthen the builder's position in price negotiations because the subcontractors have a greater stake in the company. On the other hand, if a builder becomes extremely reliant on a closely affiliated contractor, that contractor gains greater leverage with the builder and can demand higher prices for its services.

According to the survey results, home builders made no appreciable change during the housing market boom in the percentage of work they awarded their top contractors in different craft areas. Few builders in the sample relied on the top three contractors in any given area for more than 20 percent of their work. Indeed, builders in several cases reported *reducing* their use of their top three contractors by category in 2004. This may reflect either explicit choice or the impact of constrained supply in some specialty trades (electrical in particular) in certain markets.

Information sharing. Better on-site coordination requires builders to collect, analyze, and share information on construction activity. In principle, the ever-expanding availability of information and communication technologies—from cell phones, beepers, and laptop computers to handheld devices and coordination software—should dramatically reduce the price of, and increase the capacity for, such coordination. In effect, information and communication technologies provide a new means to address some of the problems of the CM model.

Survey respondents reported that the majority of subcontractors had access to information on scheduling. Overall, about 60 percent of builders provided contractors such vital information. Large divisions were more likely to provide information access than small ones, but medium-size divisions provided the greatest amount of access. Builders operating in lower-appreciation markets reported more access overall (with 69 percent of subcontractors having access to schedules versus 48 percent in higher-appreciation markets), as well as within each size group **(Figure 4.7)**.

FIGURE 4.7

Home Builders in Lower-Appreciation Markets Were More Likely to Share Scheduling Information

Divisions providing subcontractors access to schedules

Divisions (By number of homes sold in 2004)	Lower-Appreciation Markets		Higher-Appreciation Markets		All Markets	
	Number	Percent	Number	Percent	Number	Percent
Small (Under 500)	5	56	1	20	6	43
Medium (500–999)	9	82	8	62	17	71
Large (1,000 and over)	8	67	2	40	10	59
All Divisions	22	69	11	48	33	60

Source: Harvard Home Builder Study, Division Survey, 2005.

Information technologies have been used in many industries to improve coordination between businesses. The Harvard Home Builder Survey results, however, indicate that the diffusion of such technologies in residential construction was surprisingly low in 1999–2004. The largest builders in the sample did not take a significant lead in this area. For example, only about 58 percent shared detailed building plans or provided schedule changes to subcontractors, and just 37 percent drew on web-based systems for this type of coordination.[9]

Among companies with computer-based scheduling, most reported that subcontractors that were granted access used it regularly **(Figure 4.8)**. Once again, however, the size of the firm explains little about which home builders provided such information to their networks of subcontractors. Subcontractors in lower-appreciation markets appear to have used the scheduling information provided by builders at a somewhat higher overall rate.

FIGURE 4.8

Subcontractors Generally Used Scheduling Information Provided by Home Builders

Divisions whose subcontractors regularly accessed schedules

Divisions (By number of homes sold in 2004)	Lower-Appreciation Markets		Higher-Appreciation Markets		All Markets	
	Number	Percent	Number	Percent	Number	Percent
Small (Under 500)	4	80	0	0	4	67
Medium (500–999)	8	89	6	75	14	82
Large (1,000 and over)	6	75	2	100	8	80
All Divisions	18	82	8	73	26	79

Source: Harvard Home Builder Study, Division Survey, 2005.

Modern construction management requires that home builders coordinate work-site activity using a variety of mechanisms. The survey responses indicate that the tools that builders employed to do so in 2004 vary significantly. There is surprisingly little evidence of scale advantages—that is, large builders did not report systematically higher use of more advanced forms of coordination for most of the practices

9   The survey indicated that 83 percent of the largest home builders had computerized scheduling or project management capabilities versus 70 percent of the smallest home builders (these differences are not statistically significant). However, a survey conducted by the National Association of Home Builders in 2003 found that 69 percent of respondents that built 10 or fewer homes annually reported purchasing some construction supplies and materials over the Internet, but only 33 percent of those building more than 100 homes did so (Carliner 2003a). Chapter 6 discusses the comparative use of information and communication technology across builders in detail.

reviewed here. However, builders operating in markets with lower price appreciation were more likely to avail themselves of these tools than those operating in markets with higher appreciation.

PERFORMANCE AT THE CONSTRUCTION SITE

So far the discussion has focused on whether home builder size affects labor and subcontracting practices at the work site. Equally important is how home builder scale relates to operational performance. Although it does not appear that scale significantly affects adoption of advanced subcontracting or site management practices, is there evidence of the virtuous circle described in Chapter 1 in outcomes at the site?

There are many ways to measure performance at the construction site. One obviously important dimension relates to the costs of construction activity. As noted above, a variety of practices from bidding procedures to construction scheduling can affect the costs that home builders bear. The amount of time required to complete construction is a second important dimension of performance, particularly in terms of risk reduction. If builders attempt to reduce risk by building fewer homes on a speculative basis, the premium for being able to build more rapidly rises. This is in addition to the direct cost savings from having less money tied up in finished but unsold homes.

Construction costs. In many industries, scale confers cost advantages. Most people are familiar with the story of how Ford ratcheted down the cost of producing cars by redesigning the assembly process, standardizing production inputs, and taking advantage of rapid demand growth by continuing to squeeze out costs as volume increased. The virtuous circle hypothesis predicts that bigger home builders would also find opportunities to use scale to create cost advantages over competitors.

Overall, about 60 percent of total residential construction costs arise from subcontractors.[10] Of that share, outlays for framing and finish carpentry together made up about 24.6 percent of construction costs for entry-level homes in 2004 **(Figure 4.9)**.[11]

---

10 Construction costs are defined as the direct costs for building a house, not including land, overhead, and sales costs. Respondents were asked to indicate the costs associated with different crafts. In some cases, this might include the cost of materials if subcontractors were responsible for making the purchases.

11 Survey respondents reported only small changes in the percent of costs accounted for by different construction activities between 1999 and 2004. The largest increase occurred in framing costs, which rose from about 15.8 percent of total construction costs in 1999 to 17.5 percent in 2004.

FIGURE 4.9

Framing and Finish Carpentry Account for About a Quarter of Construction Costs

Average share of construction costs for entry-level homes in 2004 (percent)

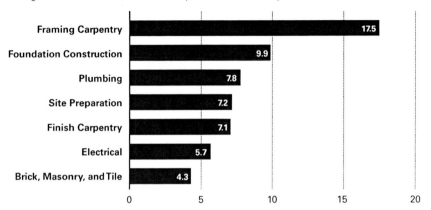

Note: Construction costs do not include the cost of land, overhead, and sales.
Source: Harvard Home Builder Study, Division Survey, 2005.

But the costs for these activities vary significantly for builder divisions of different sizes and operating in different markets. Overall, construction costs rose rather than fell with scale, with small divisions reporting an average cost of $14 per square foot for special trades subcontractor activities in 2004, compared with $22 for large divisions. This is clearly at odds with the virtuous circle argument that scale confers greater efficiency.

Moreover, overall construction costs for builders of different sizes are significantly greater in higher-appreciation markets **(Figure 4.10)**. This in part reflects the higher building costs in booming housing markets (due to tighter labor markets, higher product prices, and larger profit margins), as well as differences in the features of entry-level houses.[12] But this finding may also reflect the greater concern for cost containment among builders in lower-appreciation markets, along with their wider adoption of advanced coordination practices. Construction costs also rose modestly in inflation-adjusted terms between 1999 and 2004, particularly among the large builder divisions operating in higher-appreciation markets. Still, there is little evidence that any of the large builder divisions used their scale to reduce construction costs to any significant extent within either lower- or higher-appreciation markets.

12 Although the survey asked builders to provide estimates for entry-level homes to provide a standard basis of comparison, there is some divergence in this definition across markets. Some homes may thus contain more features and therefore have higher costs.

FIGURE 4.10

Firms of All Sizes Operating in Rapidly Appreciating Markets Reported Higher Costs for Special Trades

Average cost per sq. ft. attributed to special trades (2004 dollars)

Divisions (By number of homes sold in 2004)	Lower-Appreciation Markets		Higher-Appreciation Markets		All Markets	
	1999	2004	1999	2004	1999	2004
Small (Under 500)	8	13	12	16	10	14
Medium (500–999)	15	15	21	22	19	19
Large (1,000 and over)	19	19	21	24	20	22
All	16	16	21	22	18	19

Notes: Special trades include framing, finishing, electrical, plumbing and masonry. Includes divisions responding for both 1999 and 2004.
Source: Harvard Home Builder Study, Division Survey, 2005.

Cycle time. The rise of lean retailers like Walmart in the 1990s was fueled in large part by companies reducing the inventory costs they incurred from holding products that consumers did not want. The most successful retailers were able to provide consumers a wide range of goods while reducing their exposure to inventory risk. Similarly, the most successful suppliers to lean retailers—companies such as Procter and Gamble—provided rapid response by reducing the manufacturing time for their products (Abernathy et al. 1999).

Reducing construction cycle time also provides builders a potential competitive advantage. If home builders lower their risk by producing fewer homes on a speculative basis, they will benefit from being able to cut construction time once they receive an order. This advantage comes from reducing the direct costs of having money tied up during the construction process (whether or not the home is built on spec) and, more importantly, from reducing the risk of building homes that cannot be sold.

In terms of cycle times, the six major construction activities considered here take up a significant share of the time required to build a new house. For an entry-level home, completing these activities collectively requires 36 days—about one-third of the total construction time **(Figure 4.11)**.[13]

---

13 This is only a rough estimate since many of these activities can take place simultaneously. The overlap between activities or the downtime between stages of construction that need to be sequenced are related to the builder's effectiveness in coordinating these activities.

FIGURE 4.11

Special Trades Subcontractors Were Responsible for About a Third of the Time Required to Finish an Entry-Level Home

Average number of days spent in constructing entry-level homes in 2004

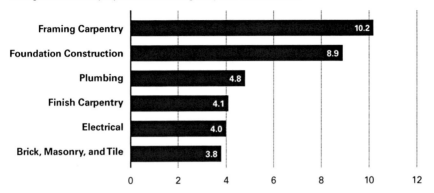

Source: Harvard Home Builder Study, Division Survey, 2005.

The amount of time required for these six basic construction activities once again varies considerably across builders and markets. Rather than big builders taking advantage of their scale to reduce cycle time, the total number of days in fact increased with division size **(Figure 4.12)**.[14] This again contradicts the virtuous circle hypothesis. Even more striking are the construction cycle times in higher- versus lower-appreciation markets, regardless of contractor size. For example, more than 10 additional days were required to complete major construction activities in a higher-appreciation market than a lower-appreciation market in 2004.

---

14 Cycle times reported here include only the time required to complete the foundation, framing, finishing, electrical, plumbing and masonry. Detailed comparisons for each trade separately are available from the authors.

FIGURE 4.12

Cycle Time Increased with the Size of the Home Builder Division
Average number of days spent on special trades

Divisions (By number of homes sold in 2004)	Lower-Appreciation Markets		Higher-Appreciation Markets		All Markets	
	1999	2004	1999	2004	1999	2004
Small (Under 500)	25.3	24.2	30.7	30.3	27.1	26.2
Medium (500–999)	27.0	32.8	52.6	47.9	38.9	39.8
Large (1,000 and over)	34.6	36.4	45.6	42.0	38.8	38.5
All	29.3	31.7	45.9	42.4	36.0	36.1

Notes: Special trades include foundation, framing, finishing, electrical, plumbing and masonry. Includes divisions responding for both 1999 and 2004.
Source: Harvard Home Builder Study, Division Survey, 2005.

Even given strong demand, tight markets, and rapid price appreciation, shorter cycle times for presold homes are still advantageous if the prices have already been specified. Shorter cycle times also increase the home builder's ability to respond to changing market conditions. It appears, however, that the gains from continuing to build new homes in rapidly appreciating markets in 1999–2004 so dominated the focus of large builders that they felt less need to invest in practices that would shorten cycle times. The long-term cost of this inefficiency has become much more apparent in the aftermath of the housing market plunge.

CONCLUSION

Building homes entails significant risks, and scale only adds to those risks, particularly where companies have gone public to seek capital for growth. Despite these forces, the results of the Harvard Home Builder Survey indicate that on-site construction practices changed little during the boom years between 1999 and 2004. In contrast to how the virtuous circle dynamic has played out in other consolidating industries, increased scale among home builders did not translate into greater production efficiencies or faster cycle times.

One explanation is that home builders simply paid attention to the easy money available from rapidly rising prices in many markets. During the housing boom, companies focused more on gaining access to and increasing their sales in markets where house prices were appreciating sharply. Reducing production costs and cycle times had lower priority because the impacts on the bottom line—at least in the short run—were smaller. What is more, the costs of addressing these issues are significant, especially in companies that have grown by acquisition. And given the longstanding traditions and practices of construction management, improving efficiency requires changing the behavior of many players—most of which are outside the home builder's direct control.

The clearest evidence that builders were following the money is found in the differences in practices in higher- and lower-appreciation markets. Divisions operating in markets with low price appreciation faced greater pressure to address problems on the cost side of the ledger. By and large, these builders paid more attention to coordination and construction practices that would reduce costs. Indeed, this attention had real impacts on performance: both construction costs and cycle times among firms operating in lower-appreciation markets were significantly below those among firms operating in higher-appreciation markets.

A related reason why large firms failed to take advantage of their scale to improve efficiency during the boom years goes back to the basic fact that home builders generally view the costs of replacing the arm's-length relationships possible in a construction management model as far greater than the benefits from more direct control of the workforce. What is interesting in the survey results is that no major home builder experimented with even small modifications of the CM model that might have improved construction cost or cycle-time performance. This reflects in part the entrenchment of that management model and the desire of large home builders to avoid activities that require closer management of workers at the job site.[15]

If home builders are to meaningfully reduce construction-related costs or the risk associated with longer cycle times, they must devise new methods to exert greater control of the construction site while continuing to act as the direct employer of only a small percentage of the workforce. As Chapter 6 discusses, home builders could achieve this through more sophisticated use of information and communication technologies. A closer relationship with contractors and subcontractors is also necessary, including a greater willingness to share data, set standards, and engage in the management of projects.

---

15 Another set of factors related to the law governing employment relationships compounds the incentives for the devolution discussed above. In particular, common law principles governing torts create peculiar incentives regarding responsibility in situations where one party contracts with another party to undertake activities. Vicarious liability refers to liability imposed upon one party because of the actions of another. Under tort law, vicarious liability may make a party liable for actions of a subordinate if that party has a "master-servant" relationship, such as an employment contract. An organization is not liable, however, if its relationship with another entity is based on a more distant, market-mediated relationship, such as by hiring the party as an independent contractor. For further discussion, see Arlen and MacLeod (2005).

5

ADVANCED OPERATIONAL PRACTICES

Unlike most manufacturing where production occurs in a controlled environment and assembly-line practices can be constantly monitored and refined, the overwhelming majority of home construction is on-site. The home building "factory" is often makeshift at best, exposed to the elements and highly labor-intensive—with only minimal capital investment to enhance the efficiency of that labor.

Builders seeking more efficient building operations would be likely to implement construction procedures that save time and money. These practices would include improving coordination with supply chain partners—including better pricing and more services—and in most instances investing in off-site preassembly of key building components. Products used in the construction process—particularly commodities like dimensional lumber, sheathing, wallboard, and concrete—are often locally sourced because transportation costs can be significant over long distances. Coordinating installation of the myriad products used over the course of the construction process therefore requires a close working relationship between the builder (or subcontractors) and their supply chains of manufacturers, distributors, and dealers.

With industry consolidation, larger home builders suddenly had the opportunity to improve their operational efficiency through a variety of advanced practices. The potential benefits of improved construction techniques were great since the starting point was so low. One leading scholar estimated that while productivity in the overall US economy (output per unit of labor) more than tripled between 1964 and 2003, it actually declined in the construction industry (Teicholz 2004).

Since home builder growth in 1999–2004 occurred principally through acquisitions rather than through internal expansion, acquired companies typically had different systems and procedures for running their operations. Standardizing practices across these newly acquired divisions therefore provided one avenue toward greater efficiency, with corporate offices able to select the best practices from a broad range of options. Furthermore, implementation costs could be spread across a larger base, reducing the expense per location.

One such productivity-enhancing strategy was to preassemble wall panels, floors, and roof trusses in more controlled environments and then deliver the components to the construction site. This operational change not only saves time and money by substituting less skilled labor in the preassembly process, but also produces homes with fewer serious construction flaws (Steven Winter Associates, Inc. 2005).

Supplier installation of home building products (also referred to as installed sales) is a related technique for achieving greater construction efficiency. This practice also helps to streamline the building process because it ensures coordination between product delivery and installation. In addition, suppliers are likely to be more knowledgeable about their products than the general construction labor force, resulting in fewer installation problems and shorter production cycles.

Improved supply chain management presented yet another opportunity that larger home builders could pursue. Even with soaring land costs during the housing boom, direct construction costs still accounted for more than half of a typical builder's expenses. According to a National Association of Home Builders study (Carliner 2003b), materials represented just over 30 percent of home builder costs in 2001, while labor contributed almost 22 percent. Indeed, delays in materials deliveries represent one of the most significant impediments to achieving labor productivity (Taylor and Bjornsson 2002).

Moreover, given their growing volume of activity in 1999–2004, larger builders could expect better pricing from suppliers and, more important, better service levels related to the timing and frequency of job-site deliveries, resolution of customer disputes, and training of employees and subcontractors. Savings on materials costs would help to lower construction costs and fatten profit margins, while enhanced services would speed up the home building process and reduce cycle times, further improving financial performance. Lower costs and shorter production cycles might therefore distinguish larger builders from their smaller competitors, who lacked comparable negotiating power.

This chapter looks at the extent to which large home builders took advantage of their growing scale to make these improvements in supply chain and materials handling productivity. After reviewing previous research on the supplier response to builder consolidation, the analysis focuses on whether larger builders were more likely to implement advanced practices related to component preassembly, supplier installation, and supply chain management to increase their operational efficiency. Results of the Harvard Home Builder Study suggest that local market conditions, rather than builder size, played the primary role in the implementation of these advanced practices.

EMERGENCE OF THE THIRD SUPPLY CHANNEL

During the 1970s and early 1980s, a new channel developed for the distribution of materials and products used for home building and residential improvements. Retail building product suppliers such as The Home Depot and Lowe's became the primary source of products for do-it-yourself homeowners, while professional dealers continued to serve custom builders and remodeling contractors. By the late 1990s, however, a third channel emerged as the larger pro dealers increasingly focused on serving high-volume home builders.

An earlier research project, the Harvard Building Products Distribution Study (Abernathy et al. 2004), found that more than half of the sales of large pro dealers (with more than $50 million in revenues in 2002) were to builders buying materials for at least 25 homes a year, while 20 percent of sales were to builders constructing more than 500 homes a year. Indeed, the share of sales by these larger dealers to higher-volume builders was up more than eight percentage points (19.8 percent vs. 11.6 percent) from five years earlier. Meanwhile, smaller pro dealers (with annual revenue of $50 million or less) became the mainstay of custom builders as well as remodeling contractors.

Focusing on big builders offered many benefits to pro dealers, not least because this customer base accounted for an increasing share of residential building material purchases each year. Concentrating on this market segment was a growth strategy that leveraged pro dealers' emerging economies of scale by shortening the distribution chain. The large building product retailers had already pioneered the manufacturer-direct distribution system that dramatically reduced the need for wholesalers. Pro dealers thus discovered that with sufficient volume, they too could deal directly with manufacturers to streamline the supply chain and reduce product costs.

Targeting big builders also helped pro dealers address the challenge of product proliferation. Residential building product manufacturers were constantly expanding their offerings to attract new customers and satisfy builders' needs. As a result, pro dealers were under pressure to increase the number of products in inventory. Indeed, the Harvard Building Products Distribution Study found that pro dealers offered 50 percent more product choices (SKUs) in 2002 than in 1997. By concentrating their business on larger builders, however, dealers could stock a more limited range of products, which in turn reduced their inventory risk. Most larger builders serve a particular market niche, often at the lower end of the home price spectrum, where they can generally offer fewer options than builders of higher-end custom and luxury homes. As a result, larger builders generally require a relatively narrow set of products.

But serving the big builder segment presented new business challenges as well. Large pro dealers reported that average gross margins from sales to larger home builders averaged 16.5 percent in 2002, compared with 24.0 percent for sales to remodeling contractors and 24.2 percent for sales to homeowners. At the same time, though, their total sales volume was generally higher because of the large quantities of purchases. In short, building materials dealers had to become more efficient in their operations to remain profitable.

Having products in stock and delivering to the job site on schedule were paramount in attracting large builders, and dealers often needed to improve their inventory management systems to support this strategy. Dealers typically needed to increase their capital investment in equipment and machinery to deliver the materials in a timely way. In addition, they often had to offer new preassembly and installation services. By 2002, 40 percent of dealers serving large builders provided prefabrication or preassembly services such as framing or panel manufacture, while 25 percent provided installation of products such as doors, windows, and roofing.

SHIFTING BUILDER PRIORITIES

By 2004, many builders had begun to pay greater attention to materials purchases. About three-quarters of respondents to the Harvard Home Builder Survey indicated that product purchasing and national accounts had increased in importance since 1999. Over that five-year period, virtually all builders implemented some corporate-negotiated pricing programs with suppliers. Well over 90 percent had corporate programs in place with some manufacturers, almost 60 percent had programs with dealers, and more than half had programs with both manufacturers and dealers (Figure 5.1).

FIGURE 5.1

Most Larger Builders Had Negotiated Better Pricing with Suppliers by 2004

Share of builders reporting corporate-negotiated pricing, volume discounts, or rebate programs (percent)

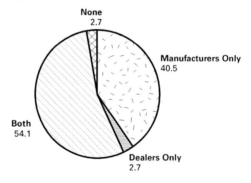

Source: Harvard Home Builder Study, Corporate Survey, 2005.

Although corporate offices became more focused on supply chain management during the building boom, most responsibilities—particularly for product selection—continued to reside at the regional or divisional level. For example, corporate offices were rarely involved in selecting commodities such as OSB/plywood/sheathing or drywall, but were likely to participate in the selection of branded products such as siding, windows, or appliances.

Given their greater involvement in product selection, builder divisions responding to the survey rated savings in purchasing and on-site construction costs as much more important than corporate offices in terms of their contribution to recent profitability **(Figure 5.2)**. Like their corporate parents, though, builder divisions felt that strong market conditions, land assembly strategies, and improved customer satisfaction were the most critical factors driving profitability.

FIGURE 5.2

Divisions Were More Likely to Cite Improved Operations as a Reason for Increased Profitability

Average rank of sources of higher profitability between 1999 and 2004
(1 = most important; 7 = least important)

	Corporate	Divisions
Strong Market/Increasing Margins	2.3	3.1
Land Assembly Strategy	3.1	2.7
Improved Customer Satisfaction	3.1	3.1
Savings in Product Purchasing	4.1	3.7
Savings in On-Site Construction Costs	4.8	4.3
Reduced Cycle Time	4.9	4.6
Increased Use of IT	5.6	6.3

Source: Harvard Home Builder Study, Corporate and Division Surveys, 2005.

But more than just better pricing, larger builders sought to use their national purchasing programs to improve the efficiency of their delivery and inventory management procedures. They also looked to materials dealers to help manage their operational risks by providing subcontractor training programs as well as installed sales and component preassembly programs.

Builders generally valued these enhanced dealer services. Almost all survey respondents reported that their dealers offered same- or next-day delivery of products, and the overwhelming majority rated this service highly. However, builders were less enthusiastic about other commonly offered services, such as customer dispute resolution and employee training programs.

Supplier installation services were also becoming more popular with builders. Of the specific products covered in the Harvard Home Builder Survey, the results show that 36 percent of divisions typically purchased OSB/plywood/sheathing installed, while 72 percent typically purchased drywall installed **(Figure 5.3)**. In addition, most builders that did not purchase these products installed would do so if the option were available. Only a small minority of builders had no interest in installed purchases, ranging from 5 percent for windows to 30 percent for OSB/plywood/sheathing.

FIGURE 5.3

Builder Demand for Installed Purchases Was Strong

Installed sales activity in 2005; share of divisional responses (percent)

	Currently Buy Installed	Would Buy	No Current Interest
OSB/Plywood/Sheathing	36	34	30
Drywall	72	17	11
Siding	59	22	19
Windows	60	35	5

Source: Harvard Home Builder Study, Division Survey, 2005.

At the same time, most large builders relied heavily on preassembled components. By 2004, almost all respondents used preassembled roof trusses for at least some of their homes, about three-quarters used preassembled floor trusses, and more than 40 percent used preassembled wall panels.

IMPLEMENTATION OF ADVANCED PRACTICES

Given these general trends, it would appear that large builders would adopt a variety of procedures to improve the management and installation of building products. Accordingly, the Harvard Home Builder Survey asked builder divisions about their specific practices in three major areas, and developed a scoring system to measure the extent of implementation.

- **Preassembly.** Advanced practices include off-site assembly of floor trusses, roof trusses, and wall panels. Builder divisions scored up to two points depending on the extent to which they used preassembly for each of these components. They also received an additional point in each category if their use of preassembly had increased over the past five years. The maximum number of points a division could receive was nine.

- **Supplier installation.** The survey also looked at the extent to which divisions purchased products on an installed sales basis, i.e., the supplier (dealer or manufacturer) provided installation services. A division received a point for each of four products (OSB/plywood/sheathing, drywall, siding, and windows) if it generally purchased that product installed. The maximum number of points a division could receive for these activities was four.

- **Supply chain management.** Advanced supply chain management practices cover a broad range of procedures related to preferred buying programs, negotiated volume discount or rebate programs, information-sharing with suppliers, and computerized or web-based purchasing and invoicing systems. A division received a point for having a preferred buying program or a negotiated volume discount or rebate program in each of the four product categories cited above; another point for having a computerized purchasing and invoicing system; and an additional point if that system was Web-based. Finally, divisions received a point if they routinely shared planned building activities with suppliers. They gained an additional point if they shared this information with suppliers with which they had a special arrangement, or an additional two points if they shared this information with all suppliers. The maximum number of points a division could receive was 13.

Overall, adoption of these advanced practices was relatively low. In 2004, the average builder division scored only about half of the total possible points in each of these areas of business operations. The adoption rates of specific advanced practices ranged from a low of 47 percent for those related to component preassembly and supply chain management, to a high of 53 percent for supplier installation.

THE ROLE OF LOCAL MARKET CONDITIONS

Central to the thesis of this study was that increased scale opened opportunities for builders to apply advanced practices across a broader base of operations, improving their efficiency and adding to their competitive advantage. Scale also provided greater access to public capital markets, allowing larger builders to make investments in advanced practices. Smaller builders, in contrast, would have had more difficulty financing these enhancements.

However, because of the decentralization that characterized most large home building firms in 1999–2004, size of corporate operations was not a decisive factor in the implementation of advanced practices. Furthermore, although the divisions of larger builders were more likely to adopt a greater share of these innovative practices, differences were generally modest **(Figure 5.4)**.[1]

FIGURE 5.4

Divisions of Larger Builders Were Only Slightly More Likely to Adopt Innovative Practices

Average adoption rates (percent)

Corporate Size (Number of homes sold in 2004)	Preassembly	Installation	Supply Chain	Overall
All Builder Divisions	46	53	47	49
Under 2,500	43	47	40	43
2,500–9,999	44	46	44	44
10,000 and Over	51	62	54	56

Source: Harvard Home Builder Study, Division Survey, 2005.

---

1   The study also considered regional location of the division as a factor, given that implementation of some innovative practices may have depended on local conditions, such as the presence of preassembly facilities or of suppliers willing to offer installation services. Again, however, there was little relationship between regional location and adoption of advanced practices.

Local market characteristics, however, strongly influenced adoption of advanced practices. In particular, divisions operating in lower-appreciation markets were more apt to purchase products from lumber and building material dealers—and, in the case of windows, more likely to purchase directly from the manufacturers—than builders in higher-appreciation markets. Divisions operating in higher-appreciation markets, in contrast, were much more apt to have subcontractors purchase the products that they installed.[2] In addition, subcontractors were far more likely to purchase drywall, regardless of market characteristics (Figure 5.5).

FIGURE 5.5

Divisions in Higher-Appreciation Markets Were More Likely to Let Subcontractors Purchase Products
Share of home builder divisions (percent)

| Product Source | OSB/Plywood/ Sheathing | | Drywall | | Siding | | Windows | |
| | Market Appreciation | | Market Appreciation | | Market Appreciation | | Market Appreciation | |
	Lower	Higher	Lower	Higher	Lower	Higher	Lower	Higher
Lumber/ Building Materials Dealer	73	40	21	0	40	16	18	4
Direct from Manufacturer	7	8	0	0	6	0	40	24
Subcontractor	21	52	67	84	30	68	15	48
Other	0	0	12	16	24	16	27	24

Notes: The total number of divisions in lower-appreciation markets is 33, and the number in higher-appreciation markets is 25. Other includes specialty dealers and wholesale distributors. Differences between higher- and lower-appreciation markets by type of distribution are significant at the 0.05 level for all product categories.
Source: Harvard Home Builder Study, Division Survey, 2005.

Apparently companies building in higher-appreciation metropolitan areas were not driven to take on the coordination challenges of buying products from local dealers or manufacturers and then arranging for installation. Instead, builders in these markets left the purchase and installation of products to subcontractors, even if this may not have been the most cost-effective strategy.

Survey results indicate that adoption of advanced supply chain management practices was correlated with local house price appreciation, although adoption of pre-

---

2   Regional subcontracting practices may also have played a role in these supply chain patterns. Some respondents indicated that it was more common practice for subcontractors in the West to purchase and install products, whereas builders in the other areas of the country typically purchased products for subcontractors to install. Many of the higher-appreciation markets in this study were in the West.

assembly and supplier installation practices was not.[3] While 60 percent of home builder divisions covered by this study were located in metropolitan areas with below-average house price appreciation in 1999–2004, more than two-thirds (68 percent) of divisions with above-average supply chain management scores were located in those same areas. Under half (49 percent) of divisions with below-average supply chain practice scores were in lower-appreciation markets. To help compensate for their smaller profit margins, divisions operating in these markets apparently negotiated more aggressively with suppliers for favorable pricing and volume discounts.

When looking only at the 19 responding divisions of the largest home builders (closing 10,000 or more homes in 2004), however, the relationships among builder size, adoption of advanced supply chain practices, and local market conditions are clearer. Fully 70 percent of the divisions of the largest firms with above-average advanced supply chain practice scores were located in lower-appreciation markets **(Figure 5.6)**. Conversely, 78 percent of divisions with below-average adoption rates operated in higher-appreciation markets.

FIGURE 5.6

Large Builders in Lower-Appreciation Markets Were Much More Likely to Implement Advanced Supply Chain Management Practices

Share of divisions of large home builders (percent)

Advanced Supply Chain Practice Score (Maximum = 13)	Lower-Appreciation Markets	Higher-Appreciation Markets	All Markets
Low (6 and under)	22	78	100 (N=9)
High (7 and over)	70	30	100 (N=10)
Total	47	53	100 (N=19)

Notes: Large builders are defined here as having sold 10,000 or more homes in 2004. Relationship between practice scores and home price appreciation levels is significant at the 0.10 level.

Source: Harvard Home Builder Study, Division Survey, 2005.

MARKET CHARACTERISTICS AND BUILDER PERFORMANCE

Given its correlation with adoption of advanced supply chain practices, house price appreciation should also be associated with builder performance measures such as production cycle time and cost of construction. Builders with more efficient operations would be expected to reduce the overall time required to construct a home by coordinating scheduling more tightly, using more preassembled and

---

3   The survey results did, however, indicate that adoption of advanced practices often depended on the availability from suppliers of services rather than on builder strategy. It is beyond the scope of this book to look at factors influencing what services suppliers offered and how those service offerings relate to local market characteristics.

supplier-installed products, and generally managing the work site more aggressively. Similarly, more efficient builders would be expected to lower their construction costs by negotiating pricing directly with manufacturers and by limiting the number of suppliers used.

However, certain factors complicate the comparison of construction cycle times and costs across builder divisions. For example, the number of subcontractors and suppliers serving a market can influence cycle time. More directly, though, the quality of new homes may vary widely across markets, affecting construction costs. Even within the entry-level category analyzed here, the quality of products used in construction can differ significantly. Companies operating in areas with high land costs (which tend to be higher-appreciation markets) are likely to build better-quality homes to keep land costs and overall sales prices more consistent.

Nevertheless, builders in higher-appreciation markets reported both longer construction cycle times and higher costs per square foot **(Figure 5.7)**. In contrast, the vast majority (71 percent) of builder divisions with below-average cycle times were located in metropolitan areas with lower house price appreciation. Cycle times for divisions in these areas were a full five days shorter than those of builder divisions operating in higher-appreciation markets.

FIGURE 5.7

Divisions in Lower-Appreciation Markets Performed Better on Basic Operating Measures

Averages across divisions in 2004

	Lower-Appreciation Markets	Higher-Appreciation Markets	All Markets
Construction Cycle Time (days)	107	112	108
Cost of Construction per Sq. Ft. (dollars)	48	58	51

Notes: Construction costs exclude basement, slab, and land. Cost differences between divisions in higher- and lower-appreciation markets are significant at the 0.15 level. Differences in cycle times are not statistically significant.
Source: Harvard Home Builder Study, Division Survey, 2005.

Home builders with lower construction costs were also more likely to be located in metropolitan areas with lower house price appreciation. Over three-quarters (76 percent) of the builder divisions reporting construction costs for entry-level homes averaging below $50 per square foot (excluding land and site preparation costs) operated in lower-appreciation markets.

Among the builder divisions with average construction costs above $50 per square foot, 59 percent were located in higher-appreciation markets (i.e., where companies might be expected to be less concerned about cost containment). Indeed, average construction costs for builders in these higher-appreciation markets were $10 per square foot above those for builders in lower-appreciation markets. As noted earlier, however, this comparison may overstate cost differences across markets because of potential disparities in the quality of materials or the level of amenities provided. Moreover, lower labor costs may have also played a role in reducing construction costs in lower-appreciation markets.

CONCLUSION

As with the management of labor, the management of materials offered large home building companies great opportunities to improve the efficiency of the construction process. During the housing boom in 1999–2004, a growing share of builders thus focused on rationalizing their supply chains and increasing their use of preassembled components.

But the nation's largest builders—who had the most to gain from implementing advanced operational practices—did not significantly outperform their midsize counterparts in this realm. Instead, it is quite likely they were simply trying to manage the rapid growth within their organizations while taking advantage of soaring housing demand. Integrating newly acquired companies into their culture and processes may well have been a lower priority at best, and a major distraction at worst—thus limiting their ability to leverage unusually favorable market conditions to become more efficient.

Similarly, regardless of the size of the corporate parent, larger home builder divisions were no more likely to implement advanced operational practices than smaller divisions. Since divisions of many of the largest firms were judged on gross margins, those operating in markets with rapidly rising prices had little incentive to reduce costs and improve efficiency.

Again, it is clear that home builders located in lower-appreciation markets had to achieve better operating performance to compete. For these companies, taking advantage of the virtuous circle through improved preassembly, supplier installation, and supply chain management practices was an important business strategy. For many of the nation's largest builders, however, efficiency was simply not a priority.

6

INFORMATION AND COMMUNICATION TECHNOLOGY

Even though home builders are generally not early adopters of advanced information and communications technologies (ICT), a starting premise of the Harvard Home Builder Study was that the operating divisions of larger companies would nonetheless be much heavier users of these systems compared with their smaller competitors. After all, these corporations faced the daunting tasks of coordinating a growing number of decentralized operations, managing numerous contractors in very different markets, and purchasing tens of thousands of products from hundreds or even thousands of home building product suppliers. It was also expected that they would most likely be users of the most advanced ICT systems available.

Much like access to capital, land assembly, and corporate branding, investing in standardized ICT systems would provide an obvious advantage for large home building firms. Scale makes these investments less expensive on a per site basis since the cost of acquisition and implementation can be spread over a larger base. At the same time, scale increases the importance of these investments given the difficulty of managing a company with dozens of geographically dispersed divisions without basic systems to ensure standard procedures.

This chapter addresses the question of whether or not large-volume home builders did in fact achieve an advantage by developing and using specialized software in their divisions, and examines how home builders used computers, specialized software, and the Internet to communicate internally as well as with customers, suppliers, and subcontractors. A separate section of the survey explored the use of ICT in divisional operations, and the results have revealed that ICT capabilities remained largely untapped within the home builder industry in 2005. Even more striking, the largest home builders were generally not out in front of their smaller competitors in implementing these systems.

Unlike other sections of the survey, the ICT portion generally asked about practices at the time the survey was sent out rather than for a comparison between 1999 and 2004 systems. Consequently, the answers reflect home builders' use of computers, software, and the Internet in mid-2005. Details concerning the size of divisions' parent companies and the level of house price appreciation in the metropolitan area where each responding division operated are presented in Appendix B.

ICT BACKGROUND

By the time the Harvard Home Builder Survey reached participants in mid-2005, personal computers were certainly used in every home builder's office—even among mid-size and small companies. The modern age of home and office computing—i.e., when computers were operated by end users—can be said to have begun in 1981 with the launch of the IBM personal computer. What drove the PC into business offices was the introduction of the spreadsheet program Lotus® 1-2-3® in 1983, specifically designed for the IBM computer. Later Microsoft's Office for Windows 95® became the largest-selling software for general office and home use.

After the introduction of the IBM PC and general office software, US sales of PCs of all brands grew dramatically. From only 0.76 million units in 1980, sales rose to 6.6 million units in 1985, to 46 million in 2000, and then to 62 million in 2005—with more than half of this number being desktop machines (eTForecasts 2011). By 2000, to maximize productivity, office PCs were likely to be connected to both a local area network (LAN) to enable internal communications, as well as to an Internet service provider (ISP) to facilitate email and other external communications.

Some US companies were worried that their workers were not taking full advantage of PCs and the Internet, and took steps to train their staffs. Others went much further than simple training. For example, the *New York Times* and *Newsweek* both ran stories in 2000 reporting that Ford Motor Company and Delta Airlines had given all of their employees (350,000 in Ford's case) free PCs with software and subsidized Internet connections as a way to ease the widespread introduction of computers and the Internet already under way in the workplace.

COMMUNICATING WITH CUSTOMERS

Although perhaps three-quarters of the US population were Internet users in 2005 (Internet World Stats 2011), large home builders do not appear to have used the Web extensively at that time except as a marketing tool. Most, if not all, of the companies responding to the Harvard Home Builder Survey maintained elaborate and easy-to-navigate Web sites targeted to potential home buyers. The sites offered information about product offerings, locations of existing and future developments, and options available from the home builder. The more sophisticated sites also provided views of floor plans and design options, and a virtual tour of different models.

While conveying the look of companies with sophisticated ICT capabilities, home builder Web sites incorporated limited use of advanced tools. In particular, very few sites offered buyers the ability to check on the progress of their homes while under construction. According to the survey results, only 30 percent of builders provided buyers with online access to the construction status of their houses. What is more, only one-third of those with this access could locate the information on the Internet.

This finding underscores a fundamental issue with builders' use of modern ICT. Providing customers with information about product offerings has been a static communication to potential buyers. As Chapter 3 showed, creating a consistent corporate brand across divisions was a priority for large home builders in 1999–2004; using the Web to convey that brand image to customers was one element of their strategy. In contrast, providing customers and suppliers with real-time updates on the current status of homes under construction would require at least daily updating of information about every home at each job site. It would also involve coordination across multiple levels within the organization as well as across multiple subcontractors and suppliers. As the following sections demonstrate, communicating this information required a level of ICT development that was largely absent among many of the large home building companies at the time of the survey.

HOME BUILDERS AND TECHNOLOGY USE IN THE BACK OFFICE

Home building requires a broad array of products. The absence of a standard language to identify these items (such as the SKUs used by retailers and their product manufacturers) makes precise product identification a challenge when placing orders. In addition, a builder typically deals with numerous suppliers, including lumber and building materials dealers, electrical distributors, plumbing supply houses, and many others that sell a myriad of specialty products. Larger builders may also deal directly with manufacturers through special national account programs as well as with local building product dealers.

Scheduling just-in-time delivery of all these products to the work site is a daunting task. Multiply that complexity by the number of models of homes in a new development, the number of communities where each division builds, and the number of divisions controlled by a single corporate parent, and the need for technological systems to manage these operations is obvious. Larger builders, who would likely benefit more from increased use of technology, and who generally have greater access to resources, were expected to show more progress in this area than smaller builders. However, as shown below, use of technology and information sharing by builders' operating divisions was generally low at the time of this survey, and divisions of larger builders rarely surpassed their smaller counterparts in their rates of utilization in such basic areas as finance and accounting, estimating costs to build homes, and coordination with subcontractors and suppliers.

Computerization of basic office operations was generally, but not always, the rule at builders at the time of this survey. Although only 2 of the 79 responding divisions reported that accounting, job cost, ledger, and payroll functions were *not* computerized at their location, a larger number of divisions reported that they had not yet computerized other back office functions. One can only conclude that the ICT revolution in the home building industry was, at best, ongoing in mid-2005.

When asked if purchase orders were computerized, 11 percent of the 80 divisions answering gave a negative response. While two-thirds of the negative responses were from divisions of mid-size firms, the low response rate prevents drawing any conclusions about the relationship between computerized purchase orders and firm size.[1] In a followup question, respondents were asked if any electronic communications were sent by EDI (Electronic Data Interchange), the then-typical (2005) Internet-based way of transmitting purchase orders along with related information exchanged between suppliers and builders.[2] Overall, 20 of the builder divisions surveyed for this study (26 percent) indicated that they were using EDI at the time of the study, while 25 (32 percent) indicated that they were not. However, 32 of the respondents (42 percent) did not know if this protocol was in use at the time of the survey. While the number of "don't know" answers to this question makes unqualified conclusions impossible, the use of the EDI protocol was clearly limited in the industry at the time of the survey.[3]

Although the overall prevalence of EDI at the time of the study is difficult to determine, it does appear that its use was somewhat less common among divisions of builders selling fewer than 2,500 homes per year, as well as divisions located in lower-appreciation markets **(Figure 6.1)**. Divisions of firms that sold fewer than 2,500 homes in 2004 were less likely to use EDI than divisions of their larger counterparts, just as one might expect given that implementing an EDI system would have been fairly expensive and therefore more likely done by a larger builder with greater resources. In addition, builder divisions located in lower-appreciation markets appear to have been somewhat less likely to have implemented EDI systems.

FIGURE 6.1

EDI Use Was Limited, Especially Among Divisions of Smaller Builders and Those Operating in Lower-Appreciation Markets

Divisions responding to the question: Do you use EDI protocol for any electronic communications?

	Corporate Size (Number of Homes Sold)			Market Type		Responses	
	Under 2,500	2,500–9,999	10,000 and Over	Lower Appreciation	Higher Appreciation	Identified Metros	All
Yes	2	10	8	8	7	15	20
No	12	4	9	14	5	19	25
Don't Know	8	10	14	10	12	22	32
Total	22	24	31	32	24	56	77

Note: In this and subsequent tables, the column labeled "All Responses" includes all division responses regardless of whether they operated in a known metro market.
Source: Harvard Home Builder Study, Division Survey, 2005.

---

1   The survey question did not restrict responses regarding how the purchase orders were sent. While they could have been sent by fax or US mail, a computer had to be used in the process.

2   For a brief description of EDI and its various forms, see http://en.wikipedia.org/wiki/ Electronic Data Interchange.

3   No other ICT survey question offered a "don't know" response, so the responses to all other survey questions are unambiguous. This allows the responses to each question to be grouped together into a single figure by reporting the percentage of "yes" responses to each question, as in Figures 6.2 and 6.3.

The limited use of EDI among home builders by 2005 stands in sharp contrast to the widespread adoption of advanced ICT elsewhere in the general residential construction sector. Most notably, the major home building product suppliers to retailers and to The Home Depot and Lowe's had long used EDI for business-to-business communication within the supply chain. Indeed, these big box retailers encouraged, if not demanded, that even their smallest suppliers use this technology.[4] It is also true that almost all items in retail stores of these major building supply retailers had individual bar codes attached, making communication about such items unambiguous in digital communications and at the checkout counter.[5]

Modern EDI software enables retailers and suppliers to continue to use invoices and purchase orders in the form each prefers; the software at each end translates the information into the necessary arrangement for Internet transmission. The software thus enables each party to do things as usual, eliminating the need for staff retraining.

HOME BUILDERS AND TECHNOLOGY USE ON THE SITE
Though the use of information and communications technology was generally quite low as of 2005, the divisions of the larger corporate builders were no more advanced than their smaller competitors in the adoption of basic systems designed to improve the efficiency of their operations on the building site. In analyzing the use of basic ICT activities covered by the Harvard Home Builder Survey, it is clear that *bigger is not necessarily better.*

When comparing ICT use by divisions of larger builders (those selling over 10,000 homes in 2004) with their smaller competitors, larger corporate builders did not have higher rates of utilization of technology for undertaking a set of activities related to the building site, such as estimating costs, providing scheduling information or sharing information on planned building activities **(Figure 6.2)**. In fact, when looking at the patterns of highlighted cells in the table (indicating the size category that had the highest rate of adoption for that measure), there appears to be very little connection between builder size and use of technology for communication and information sharing.

---

4   Early in the lean retailing revolution in 1991, a national department store CEO reported to the authors that before bar codes and EDI the company had a large office staff just to cope with advanced shipping notices and invoices from suppliers, which arrived in their offices in many sizes and formats. EDI eliminated that confusion and allowed a dramatic reduction in office staffing. The CEO noted that some of the smallest suppliers were reluctant to invest in and use EDI, but they were required to do so. Reluctant suppliers were advised to think of the investment in EDI as simply a cost of doing business with the retail store.

5   Manufacturers had found it difficult to affix a bar code to cement blocks and bricks in spite of retailers' desires. However, such manufacturers might have obtained a UPC code for each of their types of cement blocks even though no bar code, so helpful at checkout, was affixed to the items.

FIGURE 6.2

Divisions of Larger Builders Typically Did Not Make Greater Use of Available Technologies Than Their Smaller Competitors

Percent of divisions responding YES to the indicated question

	Corporate Size (Number of Homes Sold in 2004)			
	Under 2,500	2,500–9,999	10,000 and Over	All Responses
Is estimating computerized at this business location?	**77**	63	56	64
Do you have a computer-based construction cost estimating system that can produce a build price from a bill of materials?	43	**46**	24	36
Do your subcontractors and installers have access to your scheduling information?	57	43	**79**	62
Do you generally share detailed information on planned building activities with dealers/distributors and suppliers?				
Always	**48**	30	36	38
Occasionally	30	13	**42**	30

Note: The corporate size category with the greatest percentage of YES responses is in bold.
Source: Harvard Home Builder Study, Division Survey, 2005.

In contrast, technology use for on-site activities is highly correlated with local housing market conditions.[6] In particular, builder divisions in more competitive, lower-appreciation markets uniformly had higher rates of adoption **(Figure 6.3)**. Based on the experience of other manufacturing industries, adoption of each of the practices listed in the table should improve productivity at the building site. The fact that a higher percentage of builders in metro areas with lower home price appreciation adopted these processes than did those building in high price appreciation markets indicates the need for market pressure to push builders to adopt these practices. Builders in lower-appreciation markets need to be as efficient as possible to be able to compete in these low gross margin markets.

---

6   It should be noted that some respondents in the sample did not provide information on division location that allowed us to identify the respondent's metro market. The final two columns of Figure 6.3 compare responses regarding the use of technology with respect to those responses where the metro area could be identified with the total responses to the division survey including where the metro area could not be identified. The closeness in the reported percentage responding "yes" in the last two columns indicates that the group of divisions in known metro areas is an unbiased subset of the entire set of responses.

FIGURE 6.3

But Divisions Located in More Competitive Markets Were Apt to Use Technology in Their Operations

Percent of divisions responding YES to the indicated question.

	Lower- Appreciation Markets	Higher- Appreciation Markets	All Identified Metro Markets	All Responses
Is estimating computerized at this business location?	**73**	50	63	64
Do you have a computer-based construction cost estimating system that can produce a build price from a bill of materials?	**45**	24	36	36
Do your subcontractors and installers have access to your scheduling information?	**70**	50	61	62
Do you generally share detailed information on planned building activities with dealers/distributors and suppliers?				
Always	**44**	40	42	38
Occasionally	**31**	24	28	30

Note: The metro market appreciation category with the greatest percentage of YES responses is in bold.
Source: Harvard Home Builder Study, Division Survey, 2005.

Estimating costs and sharing information with suppliers and subcontractors have potentially large impacts on productivity, efficiency, and ultimately profitability. Given their importance, they warrant additional discussion.

USING TECHNOLOGY TO ESTIMATE COSTS

Similar to purchasing and invoicing, computer-based estimation of building costs is a standard computer software operation for many builders and it should be a basic operation for all home builders. Given that architects' use of computer aided design (CAD) had long been standard practice, respondents were not asked to verify this practice but rather to confirm whether the design office could go from a drawing to a computerized cost estimate before construction begins. When the survey was being developed, several large national builders said that they used such systems in all their divisions, reporting that computer-generated estimates were within a very few percentage points of actual costs. Indeed, in a private conversation, the head of a national builder's ICT unit stated that "if the estimates were not that accurate, they would likely lose their jobs."

Obviously, such software systems are enormously important tools in controlling costs, leading any observer of the home building industry to anticipate their widespread adoption. And in fact, almost two-thirds of builder divisions indicated that they used computerized estimation systems. However, it was the divisions with smaller corporate parents that were the most likely to use this tool. Some 77 percent of divisions of firms selling fewer than 2,500 homes had computerized cost estimation, compared with 56 percent of divisions of the largest builders **(Figure 6.2)**. And it was builders working in lower-appreciation markets **(Figure 6.3)** that used the software more often (73 percent) than did builders in higher-appreciation markets (only 50 percent). Cost pressures may have encouraged more builders operating in lower-appreciation markets to use computerized estimation.

Computerized estimation of costs to build homes in a particular market contributes to productivity and is therefore a plus for home builders. A separate look (not shown) of the survey responses by the size of the parent companies of the 24 divisions reporting that they used computerized estimation and operated in lower-appreciation metros revealed that a large majority (18 of 24, or 75 percent) had corporate parents that sold fewer than 10,000 homes per year in 2004. Home builders operating in the more competitive, lower-appreciation markets most likely found that computerized estimation was a more important tool to control costs than did divisions building in the higher price appreciation housing markets. There clearly remains much room for improvement in specialized software use in estimating home building costs.

USING TECHNOLOGY TO COORDINATE WITH SUBCONTRACTORS AND SUPPLIERS

At the time of the Harvard Home Builder Study, banks and brokerage firms maintained secure Web sites allowing customers online access to their accounts. These systems dramatically reduced transaction costs compared with employing trained staffs to respond to phone calls and in-person queries. It seemed reasonable to assume that home builders would accrue similar savings from creating secure Web sites to inform subcontractors about the building status of each unit at each job site. In addition, by knowing a builder's plans, suppliers could better manage their own inventory and distribution to have the right products at the right place at the right time. Nonetheless, builders generally did not have adequate systems in place to share information with their suppliers and subcontractors in a timely manner.

Home building requires continuous communications among builders, suppliers, and subcontractors to keep projects on schedule. Inside work cannot begin until the envelope is weather-tight. Insulation must go into the outer wall; plumbing, HVAC, and electrical systems have to be in place before the wallboard can be hung. Then comes a long list of inside and outside finishing subcontractors who can do their jobs only when other tasks are completed. Sharing the status of work at each site is therefore critical.

Sharing information is an easily implemented operating policy, rather than an investment decision that involves new technology and training. As a result, it appears that more of the biggest builders made the decision to share information with their subcontractors and installers. Almost 80 percent of these firms provided access to this information, compared with about half of other builder divisions.

The results were surprising. First, the expectation was that almost all builders would communicate scheduling information with all their subcontractors, but the sharing was much more restricted. The size of the parent company made a big difference in the responses. Perhaps the larger firms more clearly understood the benefits to both parties from having access to information, as well as the fact that sharing does not confer an unfair advantage to subcontractors. Meanwhile, only 19 divisions reported having production scheduling software to help coordinate on-site construction activities. Of these divisions, 11 had Web-based systems. Astonishingly, 2 of those 11 firms charged a fee to subcontractors and installers to access this information.

Sharing information about planned building activities with suppliers is generally considered critical to supply chain efficiency. If suppliers know the number of homes to be built in the near term, on-time delivery of products to the job site is much more likely. However, this practice was far from universal, even for divisions of larger builders. Specifically, almost a third of builder divisions reported that they did not usually share information about planned activity with their suppliers. In contrast, 38 percent of builder divisions always shared this information with suppliers while another 30 percent indicated that they did so occasionally. Divisions of larger builders were less likely than others to always share information on building plans with suppliers, but more likely to do so occasionally.

While builder size provides little insight into a division's decision to implement standard technologies and share information with subcontractors and suppliers, prevailing conditions in the local housing market are again more telling. As Figure 6.3 shows, builder divisions operating in lower-appreciation markets were generally much more likely to use productivity-enhancing technology, and somewhat more likely to share information with suppliers.

Computerized estimation of costs to build homes in a particular market contributes to productivity and is therefore a plus for home builders. Cost pressures may have encouraged more builders operating in lower-appreciation markets to use computerized estimation. A much larger share of divisions operating in lower-than-average home appreciation markets did so. Likewise, a larger share of divisions operating in areas with lower home price appreciation used software capable of generating cost estimates from a bill of materials.

Finally, information sharing was somewhat more widely practiced by builder divisions operating in lower-appreciation markets. While the difference was not dramatic, a higher share of divisions in low-appreciation markets reported that they always shared information with suppliers, and a higher share also reported that they occasionally shared information with suppliers. Conversely, 36 percent of divisions in higher-appreciation markets usually did not share information with suppliers compared with just 25 percent of those in lower-appreciation markets.

THE IMPORTANCE OF SHARING

Based on the experience of other major industries, the lack of information sharing with suppliers is surprising and short-sighted. Companies at all stages of the US food supply chain, for example, have benefited from sharing data regarding final consumer sales. Sales data collected at the cash register allow retailers to reduce their exposure to unsold inventory, while the provision of that information to suppliers help them to plan and produce more efficiently. There is no reason the same benefits could not accrue to home builders or their major suppliers.

The failure to take advantage of such benefits may again point to organizational barriers arising from not integrating acquired units or being willing to incur the costs of standardizing practices across divisions. The reluctance to overcome these barriers only if required (rather than in recognition of the potential benefits from information sharing) is illustrated by the fact that of those builders responding that they did not share information with suppliers, two-thirds indicated that they would share this information if they were requested to do so. Hedging even more were an additional 12 percent that indicated that it would "depend on the situation" **(Figure 6.4)**.

FIGURE 6.4

Most Builders Shared (or Would Have Shared) Information on Planned Building Activity with Suppliers

Divisions Sharing Information (percent)

Divisions that Would Share If Asked (percent)

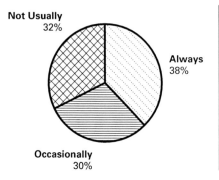
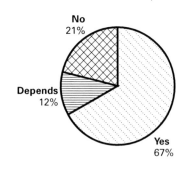

Note: Divisions that would share if asked are of those divisions responding "not usually" to the question of whether they shared information on planned building activity with suppliers.
Source: Harvard Home Builder Study, Division Survey, 2005.

Builder divisions in markets with lower home price appreciation were more likely to share information with suppliers than those operating in higher-appreciation areas **(Figure 6.5)**. Once again, there is a clear relationship between information sharing and local market conditions.

FIGURE 6.5

Builders in Lower-Appreciation Markets
Were More Likely to Share Information

	Lower-Appreciation Markets		Higher-Appreciation Markets		All Markets	
	Number	Percent	Number	Percent	Number	Percent
Generally Share Planned Building Activity	24	75	16	64	40	70
Share Plans With All Dealers and Suppliers	18	56	9	41	27	50
Provide Subs and Installers Access to Schedule	23	70	12	50	35	61

Note: Differences are not significant at the 0.05 level.
Source: Harvard Home Builder Study, Division Survey, 2005.

Indeed, information sharing among builders in lower-appreciation markets often extended to allowing subcontractors access to their future building plans and schedules. Phone/fax seems to have been the dominant method of notifying subcontractors of schedule changes (but the response rate was too low to determine the extent to which subcontractors or suppliers were informed). Only 43 percent of 79 respondents provided daily status reports on homes at a given job site, while another 43 percent updated home status at least once a week. Builder divisions used a variety of methods to communicate construction status to subcontractors and suppliers, with just over a third (37 percent) posting updates on the Internet. As noted previously, in 2005 several builder divisions surprisingly required subcontractors and material suppliers to pay a monthly fee to access the builders' Web sites to learn the construction status of a given home. Nonetheless, the experience of builders in lower-appreciation markets suggests that information sharing with other parties can be done if there is a will to do so.

FACTORS DISCOURAGING GREATER USE OF TECHNOLOGY

Often, the limited use of standard information and communicating technologies by builders reflected prevailing conditions in the industry in 2005. For example, even if home builders had invested in e-commerce systems during this time, few building product suppliers offered this communication option. Results from the earlier Harvard Building Products Distribution Study indicated that the use of e-commerce by lumber and building materials dealers, specialty dealers, wholesale distributors, and manufacturers had at best just begun at that time (Abernathy et al. 2004). Only 36 percent of builder divisions that used lumber and building materials dealers as their primary source of one or more major product lines reported the availability of e-commerce capabilities—the same share among builders that primarily went direct to manufacturers for some products **(Figure 6.6)**. These shares are well above those of specialty dealers or wholesale distributors.

FIGURE 6.6

Most Suppliers Did Not Offer E-Commerce Capabilities to Builders in 2004

Share of divisions reporting that e-commerce capabilities are offered (percent)

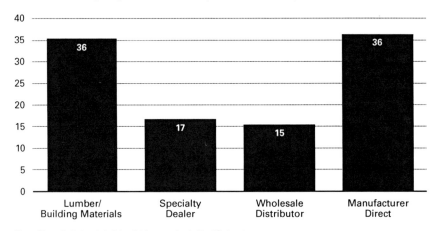

Note: Shares include only builder divisions serving in identified metro areas.
Source: Harvard Home Builder Study, Division Survey, 2005.

Another reason why all divisions of the largest home builders did not have uniformly computerized processes is that most of these companies had grown quickly by acquisitions and therefore had to contend with numerous legacy systems. They frequently did not have the time or willingness to standardize systems across divisions. Clearly, great opportunities existed at the time for builders to use advanced software packages for applications such as projecting costs for homes before construction began. As mentioned, almost half of the respondents to the Harvard Home Builder Survey operating in more competitive markets were doing just that, compared with about a quarter operating in less competitive markets.

Accurate cost estimation depends on having current information on local labor and building material costs. The use of such information with the estimating software would have improved many divisions' financial performance. But the survey results indicate this was not always the case. In response to the question of whether most product costs were electronically shared between the company's procurement system and its estimating system, only 34 percent of the surveyed divisions responded at all. Of those, about 70 percent indicated they had such systems.

In summary, implementation of basic computer systems at home building divisions was limited at the time of the survey **(Figure 6.7)**. Again, the largest home builders were not industry leaders in adopting these systems. Companies selling 10,000 or more homes a year had the financial resources to devote to these initiatives, especially during the housing boom years. Even so, they had essentially the same or lower implementation rates as companies selling fewer than 2,500 homes a year. Divisions of the largest parent companies, which could have used computers to leverage their economies of scale in local markets, were less likely to have implemented these systems than divisions of smaller parent companies. The most positive finding is that builders reporting higher frequency of use were operating in lower-appreciation markets, where competition forced divisions to be as efficient as possible.

FIGURE 6.7

Many Builder Divisions Had Not Yet Computerized Back Office Functions in 2004

Share of builder divisions using computerized business systems (percent)

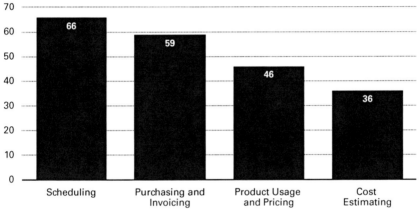

Source: Harvard Home Builder Study, Division Survey, 2005.

CONCLUSION

In other consolidated industries, the largest firms—whether collectively or individually—led the change in information and communications technology. For example, a group of leading grocery producers, suppliers, and supermarket retailers got together in late 1969 to develop a common product identifier, which led to bar coding and its use first in food stores (Brown 1997; Abernathy et al. 1999; Haberman 2001). In another case, The Home Depot and Lowe's enforced bar coding of home building products and required the use of EDI for communications with suppliers.

Such leadership within the home building industry in the realm of ICT was still absent in 2005. At that time, builder divisions were slow to adopt computer systems to help with many back-office functions, and still fewer had the software necessary to estimate the cost of building a given home design with a bill of materials. The use of electronic scheduling software was also relatively rare.

Home builder divisions operating in the most competitive markets—metro areas with below-average home price appreciation—were more likely to use advanced ICT systems than divisions building in the more profitable markets with higher home price appreciation. For example, in these more competitive markets, it was the smaller corporations (selling fewer than 2,500 homes) whose divisions were most likely to use computerized cost estimation.

Contrary to expectations, the largest home builders did not use their market power to drive ICT changes in their construction operations and to achieve operating efficiencies. Few developed and implemented specialized software throughout their companies or used the Internet to coordinate with subcontractors, suppliers, and installers. While the largest builders did share information with subcontractors more often than their smaller competitors, such practices were far from universal in 2005.

7

LESSONS ABOUT BUILDER SCALE
AND PERFORMANCE

The preceding chapters looked in detail at the relationship between home builders' scale of operations and their adoption of innovative building practices. After a careful evaluation, particularly of the nation's largest companies, it is clear that although scale and performance are linked along several dimensions, the basic finding that bigger does not necessarily mean better remains.

Large home builders did take advantage of their size in terms of access to capital, land assembly, and corporate branding. In these areas, being bigger did yield important benefits. However, little connection was found between home builder scale and adoption of innovative practices in the areas of labor coordination, use of pre-assembly and other major productivity-enhancing building methods, supply chain management, and information technology and communications systems.

In many respects, this conclusion could be anticipated from responses to the corporate portion of the Harvard Home Builder Survey. Few corporate-level participants attributed their financial success during the 1999–2004 housing boom to efficient on-site operations, cost savings from suppliers, or better information technology systems. Similarly, few stated that these functions became a higher priority at corporate offices during the survey period. Given the market conditions at hand, it is understandable that home builders focused on the functions that helped them achieve greatest profitability.

Still, given the experience of other major industries that had undergone significant consolidation, it seemed reasonable at the outset of this study to expect that some large builders would innovate in these operational areas and reap additional longer-term financial rewards as a result. Instead, the survey results show that larger builders did not take the lead in implementing advanced building practices and were often outperformed by their smaller competitors on these measures.

This chapter explores some of the possible explanations for this finding. The first is that bigger builders operate more like a federation of small independent companies rather than as a single entity. As such, they have limited ability centrally to implement, much less benefit from, scale economies. The chapter then assesses whether big builders even attempted to implement operational efficiencies as a benefit of scale. An underlying assumption at the outset of this study was that large builders would leverage their size to improve their home construction practices, which in turn would increase profitability.

As it turns out, builders did not perceive that many of the traditional benefits of scale economies were critical to profitability during the housing market boom. Indeed, large builders found easier ways to increase their margins by focusing on the revenue rather than the cost side of their ledgers, such as increasing their levels of production or operating in land-constrained markets. In an environment of double-digit home price appreciation, big builders likely saw the costs of standardizing the practices of acquired companies as too high relative to the benefits.

Given the lack of relationship between home builder size and operational efficiency, the discussion then turns to the types of firms that did implement innovative practices in 1999–2004. As previous chapters have demonstrated, local house price appreciation was often more closely associated with operational performance than builder size, whether measured from a corporate or divisional perspective. Moreover, better financial performance was more closely linked to housing market characteristics than to operational performance.

CHALLENGES OF IMPROVING OPERATIONAL PERFORMANCE

During the time of the Harvard Home Builder Study, large home building companies had divisions in multiple metropolitan areas throughout the United States. Along with different housing styles and consumer preferences, each of these markets had its own land entitlement procedures, building codes, labor arrangements, and economic conditions. The fact that larger builders were rapidly acquiring other companies compounded the effects of all these differences. Indeed, the National Association of Home Builders concluded that increases in the share of homes completed for sale by the top 10 home builders from 1994 to 2005 were due, in a large part, to the companies' growth by acquisition and not by internal growth.

Big builders' acquisitions strategies, however, created a major obstacle to reaping the benefits of scale. These home builders still acted as federations of local companies rather than as integrated organizations. Most corporations—whether in home building or other sectors—wrestle with the difficulty of merging acquired units with distinct operational practices, personnel, internal incentive systems, and cultures.[1] Integration is all the more difficult if the acquired units face different types of competitive environments. For a complex activity like home building, achieving true organizational integration requires time and significant effort.

---

1   One of the best-known examples is General Motors, which grew in the 1920s and 1930s from the merger of several car companies. Alfred P. Sloan, the CEO of GM from 1923 to 1946, is remembered for forging the national auto giant from many divergent companies, thereby gaining both operational efficiencies and national marketing capabilities while also taking advantage of the product variety afforded by the mergers. See Sloan (1963).

During the heyday of rapid growth in 1999–2004, it appears from responses to the Harvard Home Builder Survey that large builders found it particularly difficult to implement uniform and efficient home building procedures across multiple divisions. But that was only part of the reason that larger builders did not perform better operationally than their smaller counterparts. In fact, the survey results reveal little connection—and, in some cases, an inverse relationship—between operational efficiency and financial performance within the home building industry.

In retrospect, the reasons why seem clear. Builder divisions with the largest gross margins on homes sold in 2004 were generally located in housing markets where consumer demand outstripped the ability of builders to produce new homes, fueling price appreciation. In these markets, builder operating performance was less than spectacular given that they had little incentive to improve their operations because their large margins were not directly linked to efficient practices. The top 10 percent of builder divisions in terms of gross margins had only average construction cycle times, below-average construction costs, and below-average customer satisfaction scores. At the same time, reflecting the strong demand in these high-margin markets, the sales prices of their entry-level homes were almost 50 percent higher than the average across all divisions covered in the study **(Figure 7.1)**.

FIGURE 7.1

The Best Financial Performers Were
Less Efficient in Their Operations

Division averages for entry-level homes weighted by 2004 sales

	Top 10% of Divisions for Gross Margins	Bottom 10% of Divisions for Gross Margins	All Divisions
Gross Margins (percent)	34.2	13.2	22.6
Cycle Time (days)	102.4	87.4	103.1
Construction Costs per Sq. Ft. (dollars)	49.7	39.2	54.4
Customer Satisfaction (percent willing to recommend)	84.7	83.5	87.3
Average Sales Price (dollars)	295,000	195,000	199,000

Source: Harvard Home Builder Study, Division Survey, 2005.

For builders able to achieve large margins, the benefits of cutting construction costs or cycle time paled in comparison to the additional profits they were able to command by increasing production volume. On the contrary, any short-term disruption of normal operations that may have resulted from implementing more efficient procedures would likely have been counterproductive to meeting short-run financial goals.

At the other extreme, builder divisions with the smallest gross margins generally reported above-average operating performance. These divisions had shorter cycle times, lower construction costs, and slightly below-average customer satisfaction ratings. Again, reflecting local market conditions, the prices of homes sold by these divisions were near the average for all builder divisions.

THE IMPORTANCE OF LOCAL MARKETS REVISITED

The preceding chapters have repeatedly emphasized the relationship between local housing market characteristics and builder performance. Indeed, in most instances it is only possible to identify the impact of scale when looking through the lens of specific market characteristics. For example, while larger builders generally reported somewhat more aggressive land practices, larger builder divisions in higher-appreciation markets scored significantly higher on this measure. Aggressive land positions were much more likely to generate positive financial results in markets where house prices were rising rapidly. Builders that controlled land in markets where demand for new homes was strong were in a better position to reap significant financial benefits than their less aggressive competitors.

In the realm of supply chain management, the size of builder operations made little difference to the adoption of advanced practices. But when combined with market conditions, the impact was dramatic: larger builders located in lower-appreciation markets had significantly higher adoption rates, which in turn yielded better operational performance. While it is important to note that home quality may differ across metropolitan areas, builders in lower-appreciation markets were able to achieve below-average construction costs and cycle times. In other words, when market conditions were more competitive, builders were forced to be more efficient in their operations.

Builders operating in lower-appreciation markets were also better at coordinating with their supply chain partners. These divisions were more likely than their counterparts in higher-appreciation markets to share information on building plans with suppliers and to ensure that their subcontractors and installers had access to building schedules. Similar results were observed in other operational areas, with divisions in lower-appreciation markets more likely to use computerized cost estimating systems and provide daily updates on the status of homes under construction.

Despite demonstrably better operating performance, however, builders in lower-appreciation housing markets lagged their competitors in higher-appreciation markets on key financial measures. Their gross margins on homes sold in 2004 averaged more than 500 basis points below those of builders in higher-appreciation markets, while their net income averaged more than 900 basis points below. At least during the period covered by the Harvard Home Builder Survey, the benefits of improved efficiency did not come close to matching the advantages of operating in metros with higher home price appreciation **(Figure 7.2)**.

FIGURE 7.2

Builders in Lower-Appreciation Markets Performed Less Well on Financial Measures than Those in Higher-Appreciation Markets

Median responses by divisions

2004	Lower-Appreciation Markets	Higher-Appreciation Markets	All Markets
Gross Margins (percent)	20.0	25.0	22.0
Net Income (percent)	8.0	17.8	10.4
Land Controlled (years)	4.3	5.0	4.8
Average Sales Price (dollars)	158,000	281,000	178,000

Notes: The table includes only divisions operating in identifiable metro areas. The responses for "All Markets" differ from the responses for "All Divisions" in Figure 7.1 because they include divisions operating in regional markets and outside identifiable metro areas. Land controlled is measured as the number of years that land owned or optioned would accommodate projected production levels.
Source: Harvard Home Builder Study, Division Survey, 2005.

DISENTANGLING THE EFFECTS OF SIZE AND LOCATION

Along with local market conditions, it is clear that a corporate parent's policies and procedures have impacts on the financial and operating performance of home builder divisions. Using the analysis of variance (ANOVA) technique, it is possible to sort out which of these factors had a significant effect on builder performance, and how much of the variability in performance is attributable to each factor. For example, the analysis looks at whether the financial performance of a builder division located in a particular metropolitan area was closely associated with the fact that that division was doing business in that specific area. The technique involves comparing the variation in reported gross margins across divisions operating within specific metro areas with the variation in average gross margins for builders in all metro areas. The dimension that has significantly less variation is thus more closely associated with gross margins.

In the metrics analyzed in this study, the performance of builder divisions within a given metropolitan area was more consistent than performance across metro areas. As a result, knowing the location of the home builder division reveals a lot about the expected performance of that particular divisional operation **(Figure 7.3)**.

FIGURE 7.3

Division Performance Was More Consistent Within the Same Metro Area than Across Metro Areas

Average sum of squares of difference between individual observations and group average

	Within-Metro Average	Cross-Metro Average	Dimension with Greater Consistency
Gross Margins (percent)	25.6	66.8	Within Metros
Cycle Time (days)	678.6	1714.3	Within Metros
Costs per Sq. Ft. (dollars)	94.5	219.3	Within Metros
Land Controlled (years)	2.5	9.6	Within Metros
Homes Presold (percent)	691.1	1398.1	Within Metros

Notes: Variations between within-metro and cross-metro averages are statistically significant at the 0.05 level. Outliers were removed from cost per sq. ft. and land controlled analyses. Construction costs are used as a measure of builder efficiency, although differences may also relate to the quality of building products used across markets. Land controlled is measured as the number of years that land owned or optioned would accommodate projected production levels.
Source: Harvard Home Builder Study, Division Survey, 2005.

A similar analysis looked at whether knowing the corporate parent also provided insight about a division's performance. In this case, the results were less conclusive. For construction cycle time and number of years of land controlled, the variation within individual builder divisions was less than the variation across all builders. For these two measures, knowing the builder would provide some insight about what to expect in terms of performance. For the other measures, however, there was no statistical difference between the performance of divisions of the same parent company and the average across all builders **(Figure 7.4)**.

FIGURE 7.4

Divisions of Different Builders Operating Within the Same Metro Area Performed More Consistently than Divisions of a Single Company

Average sum of squares of difference between individual observations and group average

	Within-Builder Average	Cross-Builder Average	Dimension with Greater Consistency
Gross Margins (percent)	14.2	37.4	Difference Not Significant
Cycle Time (days)	532.4	1454.6	Within Builder
Cost per Sq. Ft. (dollars)	82.7	44.7	Difference Not Significant
Land Controlled (years)	5.2	10.1	Within Builder
Homes Presold (percent)	590	791.4	Difference Not Significant

Notes: Variations between within-builder and cross-builder averages are statistically significant at the 0.05 level; differences are otherwise reported as not significant. Outliers were removed from cost per sq. ft. and land controlled analyses. Construction costs are used as a measure of builder efficiency, although differences may also relate to the quality of building products used across markets. Land controlled is measured as the number of years that land owned or optioned would accommodate projected production levels.
Source: Harvard Home Builder Study, Division Survey, 2005.

Most performance metrics for builder divisions doing business within a given housing market showed relatively little variation, while most metrics for builders serving multiple metro areas varied significantly more. These results imply that it is possible to learn more about the likely performance of a builder division by knowing where it operated than by knowing its corporate parent. Knowing that a builder division operated in the Atlanta area, for example, provides some expectations about how it would perform operationally. Conversely, knowing the corporate parent of that builder division provided much less insight into likely operational performance.

CAN BIGGER GET BETTER?

These findings reinforce the conclusion that major home builders were understandably more focused on short-term profits during the housing boom than on longer-term operational efficiency. The choice for builders perhaps came down to tackling the difficulty of implementing standardized procedures across highly decentralized operations, or taking a more pragmatic approach by allowing each division to operate with the tools and procedures they had in place. Change is challenging even for organizations that start as a single entity; it is even more complicated for companies—like most of the country's largest home builders—that have grown through acquisitions. Overlay that on unprecedented revenue growth driven by soaring house prices, and it is easy to see why efficiency did not take priority.

Now that the housing bubble has burst and conditions are much more competitive, what are the prospects that large home builders can gain the advantages of scale implied by the virtuous circle? The greatest opportunities lie in areas where creating corporate standards and practices will lower costs, improve efficiency, and diffuse best practices. These areas include the use of information technology for the home building industry and certain supply chain management practices such as creating internal systems for product identification and tracking. The barriers to making these improvements are largely internal and involve breaking out of institutional inertia to standardize management information systems and administrative procedures. Although the initial costs of this undertaking may be high, the future financial rewards are likely great.

Other potential improvements face more formidable obstacles because they are linked to both internal operations and established practices within specific home building markets. These practices relate to how companies hire and coordinate subcontractors, manage the construction process, handle materials purchases, and take advantage of production innovations such as preassembly. For example, subcontractors in some areas of the country bid projects to include the required construction products (marking up their cost), which generally eliminates potential savings to be gained from corporate purchasing policies. Such longstanding practices can be difficult to change.

Large home builders have, however, demonstrated that they can successfully implement company-wide policies despite their highly decentralized structure. As Chapter 3 showed, many respondents to the Harvard Home Builder Survey invested substantial resources into brand building and improved customer satisfaction. To create a consistent customer experience, companies must standardize design and product options, develop design requirements and building quality standards, and establish protocols for interactions with customers, to name but a few of the requisite policies. Clearly, companies made brand awareness and customer satisfaction priorities in the early 2000s and seem to have been successful at implementing consistent policies across their divisions. This implies that home builders can make similar corporate changes to standardize divisional procedures in other operational areas.

In the aftermath of the housing crash, large home builders must weigh the costs of moving away from their federation-style structure against the benefits of adopting company-wide operational innovations. During the prolonged building boom—and particularly at its peak—the potential benefits were insufficient relative to their costs to justify change. Given current conditions and likely prospects for the future, however, home builders must reevaluate this tradeoff. As the following chapter explains, big builders can look to examples of other consolidated industries to discover effective ways to capture the benefits of scale.

8

GAINING ADVANTAGE FROM SCALE

Only if the collective physical facilities and human skills were carefully coordinated and integrated could the [modern] enterprise achieve the economies of scale and scope that were needed to compete in national and international markets and continue to grow.
~ Alfred D. Chandler, *Scale and Scope: The Dynamics of Industrial Capitalism,* p. 594.

Home builder consolidation was one of the most visible changes accompanying the extended housing market boom that began in the mid-1990s. Near the peak of the home building cycle in 2004, large builders had leveraged their scale to access capital, acquire land and manage development, and brand their products to market their homes to customers. But contrary to expectations that builders' enhanced market power would also lead to innovation and operational efficiencies, improved performance, and further market expansion, there is little evidence that bigger meant better. Big builders did not leverage their scale into operating advantages in these areas.

The absence of systemic improvements in operations—including construction coordination, labor practices, information technology, project planning, and supply chain management—both raises red flags and underscores opportunities. With housing markets still depressed after the severe economic recession, it has never been more important for home builders to act upon any of these opportunities that they have so far overlooked. As the preceding chapters explain, however, this requires changing their highly decentralized organizational structure—a significant challenge given the involvement of so many other actors in the home building process, including suppliers, subcontractors, regulatory agencies, consumers, and local workforces.

While some builders did in fact implement more efficient practices during the housing boom, innovations were often restricted to housing markets where relatively low home price appreciation forced greater competition, which in turn required firms to focus on costs. To compete and prosper in the years ahead, more home builders should, and will, adopt these practices more widely. Drawing on the lessons from other consolidated industries that have grappled with similar problems, this chapter lays out several ways that home builders can leverage their scale to boost their operating performance and, in turn, their profitability.

IMPROVE SUBCONTRACTOR COORDINATION AND WORKFORCE QUALITY

Many industries have moved toward the construction management model in that they rely more and more on other organizations to perform work that is outside the company's core competencies. This trend has been characterized in a variety of ways, including outsourcing, contracting out, and de-verticalization. In all cases, it involves moving aspects of the production process outside the traditional boundaries of the firm to other businesses that undertake this work. For example, Apple Computer focuses on research, new product development, final product design, and product marketing, leaving actual production of the iPhone, iPod, iPad, and other products to a network of subcontracting suppliers and a final assembler. Similarly, the use of modular subassemblies in the aerospace and automobile industries is also well established. For their part, financial institutions, airline reservation offices, and customer support centers of computer manufacturers farm out many backroom activities—such as transactions processing and call center operations—to other companies that are often located outside of the United States.

Indeed, reducing labor costs through the use of outsourcing, subcontracting, and related methods of "fissuring" the employment relationship has become widespread practice (Weil 2010). Shifting employment to other units that produce goods or provide services does, however, come with risks. Coordinating a network of suppliers in dispersed locations can lead to design and quality problems, increase work-in-process inventories, and raise the risk of production delays or even stoppages.[1] If the lead firm is particularly concerned about the reputation of its products or services, the failure of key suppliers to meet quality standards or reconcile designs can be devastating—as Toyota recently discovered in regard to manufacturing of the Prius and other models.

Successfully subcontracting or outsourcing work therefore requires attention to coordination, quality control, monitoring, and support and training. Although ICT and related technologies have made it easier to do so, failure to create institutional support for these practices can impose huge costs and risks on businesses.

At the same time, a host of industry-based studies have found that "high-road" human resource policies, when integrated with advanced manufacturing techniques, can significantly boost productivity while also improving labor force wages and working conditions (Pfeffer 1998; Ichniowski et al. 2000; Lazonick 2009). By combining innovative methods such as team-based production and just-in-time assembly with quality control circles, labor-management initiatives, and other forms of employee engagement, companies in a variety of manufacturing industries have been able to increase firm performance and earnings, job quality, and other workforce

---

1   In 2009 NCR Corporation, GE, and Dow Chemical all announced decisions to move some of their outsourced production back to the United States in part because of delays and production problems. Boeing has also had quality problems with distant suppliers of sections of its new plane, the Dreamliner.

outcomes (Appelbaum and Batt 1995). Certain service-based industries also adopted these innovations in the latter part of the 1990s and after 2000. These approaches stand in contrast to "low-road" policies that focus on reducing labor costs through practices that put pressure on wages, reduce employee benefits, and downplay the importance of investing in human capital (Shulman 2003; Greenhouse 2008).

Application to home building. The construction management model has been—and will likely remain—the basic model in home building. One of the downsides of this approach is that it prevents builders from taking greater advantage of their scale to bid work, schedule and manage subcontractors, and ensure access to a quality workforce.

Under the construction management model, subcontractors employ most workers. As a result, the ability of subcontractors to recruit, compensate, and manage their workforces potentially affects home builder performance. The home builder's "big picture" perspective on the overall project thus cannot necessarily remedy a subcontractor's inefficiency. For example, single-family housing production uses far less capital equipment than other construction sectors, in part because of the relatively low wages that subcontractors pay their workers. This practice reduces the incentives to invest in productivity-enhancing technologies,[2] which in turn prevents the subcontractor base from performing in the most efficient or well-coordinated ways. Similarly, subcontractors' low-wage/low-skill employment strategy—often relying on an undocumented immigrant workforce—often results in high turnover. This not only reduces subcontractors' incentives to invest in the skills training required to develop innovative construction approaches, but also limits their ability to maintain a reliable and productive workforce.[3]

Applying the lessons of high-road employers from manufacturing and other sectors would mean changing established subcontracting practices to increase these incentives and require home builders to play a more active role in worker recruitment, supervision, and training. At the extreme, home builders would have to directly employ more of the workforce, especially in the basic trades involved in many phases of residential construction. This would provide home builders greater incentive to develop a core group of workers with skills and training in the area of construction coordination, and increase the possibility of creating more efficient operational practices that could be transferred across divisional boundaries to improve costs and reduce cycle times. This could also lead to better workplace outcomes in residential construction more generally in terms of wages, benefits, and safer working conditions.

---

2   This can be illustrated by comparing earnings of workers in residential and non-residential construction. Based on estimates from the US Bureau of Labor Statistics, Current Employment Statistics survey, the average hourly earnings for workers in residential construction in 2008 were $19.47—almost 19 percent lower than the $23.10 average for workers in the non-residential sector (commercial, industrial, and heavy and highway construction).

3   Another impediment relates to tort liability and the doctrine of vicarious liability. The master-servant relationship (a common law concept regarding the relationship between a principal and an agent in the production of a good) between home builders and subcontractors potentially exposes home builders to greater liability than if subcontractors were deemed independent contractors. However, maintaining this distance undermines home builders' ability to improve coordination at the construction site.

Yet even without directly hiring more workers, large home builders could improve labor force quality and conditions in ways that would increase efficiency. One approach would be to modify their relationship with key subcontractors. The Harvard Home Builder Survey results indicate that large home builders awarded a relatively constant share of work to their top three contractors in different trades and markets between 1999 and 2004. In other industries that have made supply chain and assembly innovations, however, companies have limited the number of their key suppliers. For example, the lean retailers—Walmart, Target, and Macy's—have substantially reduced the number of suppliers they use in critical product areas. Similarly, manufacturers such as Ford, Toyota, and Dell Computers have cut the number of companies providing subassemblies. Moving toward a smaller number of vendors provides the selected suppliers and subcontractors a greater stake in the relationship, thereby enhancing the benefits of collaboration and workforce investment.

As experience in other sectors also shows, relying on a smaller group of key subcontractors can still be done using competitive bidding processes and ensuring that suppliers have incentives to meet high standards over time. In addition, successful subcontractors receiving a larger share of work would have greater incentives to invest in their workforces as well as in more advanced construction technologies. This in turn could result in lower turnover, improved productivity, and higher quality—a virtuous circle in human resources to complement those in other areas.

Although the Great Recession has largely eliminated the problem of shortages in key trades, there are two reasons why labor pressures will return once the market recovers. First, much of the labor force drawn upon during the home building boom was made up of immigrants, many of whom were undocumented workers from Mexico and Latin America (Kochhar 2006). The ongoing debate about immigration policy will largely determine the availability of these workers in the coming decade.

Second, Harvard Home Builder Survey respondents indicated that they were concerned about finding qualified workers in skilled trades—particularly electricians and plumbers. This shortage arises from a basic characteristic of residential construction. Contractors require a workforce capable of performing skilled tasks. Because of constantly changing demand, however, firms employ only a core group of workers and call upon additional labor depending on the number of projects under way. The high variability of labor demand reduces the benefit for these companies to invest in training (beyond its key workers).[4]

Craft training is also general rather than firm-specific, allowing workers to carry the skills acquired in one job to other projects. The portability of skills means that construction firms have a further disincentive to invest in training. Absent unions, which

---

4   The labor/management apprenticeship system in the commercial, industrial, and public construction sectors arose in response to this problem. Typically, a joint labor/management fund finances and administers apprenticeship programs for an area. All signatory contractors pay into the apprenticeship fund, based on hours of work. Local apprentice programs are often supplemented by regional and international union programs that attempt to standardize and upgrade curricular materials and provide support for training. Apprenticeship programs remain one of the competitive advantages of unions in other construction sectors (Dunlop 1993; Weil 2005).

have helped to solve this problem in the other parts of the construction industry, the relative lack of skilled trades workers will remain a bottleneck in the residential sector if the onus of hiring remains on subcontractors.[5]

INCREASE STANDARDIZATION AND PREASSEMBLY OF COMPONENTS

In the early days of the automobile industry, assembly relied primarily on crafts-men using files and hammers to adapt the heavy sheet-metal parts to fit. Henry Ford recognized that for parts from different suppliers to assemble smoothly, it was necessary to set standards for parts measurement. He even sent standard-gauge blocks to each supplier to be sure that measurement of one inch was the same in every factory.

The personal computer industry has also benefited greatly from open architecture and industry standards. PC suppliers have continued to expand the scope of their subassemblies to the point that manufacturers no longer make any of the parts for their computers. Major brands such as Apple, Dell, and HP develop the overall de-signs, while subcontractors provide the parts or subassemblies such as hard drives and monitors. Indeed, the named PC makers are unlikely to perform the final as-sembly. The end product is nevertheless a distinctive, branded computer with all the special features and characteristics recognized by the buying public.

In addition, manufacturers in the automobile and aerospace industries draw in-creasingly on modular production methods. Suppliers are assigned key component groups to design and assemble. For example, Ford and Toyota both rely on sup-pliers to design, engineer, and produce steering systems that are then integrated into the automobile at a late stage of assembly. Similarly, Boeing Corporation has never built engines for its planes but instead participated in setting jet engine design requirements with the Pratt and Whitney division of United Technologies, GE, and Rolls-Royce. In this way, suppliers become co-developers that work closely and interactively with the manufacturer. These arrangements allow companies to har-ness the expertise and experience of their suppliers, thereby enhancing productiv-ity, quality, and innovation (Womack, Jones, and Roos 1991; MacDuffie and Helper 1997; Pil and MacDuffie 1996).

Application to home building. Home builders have long benefited from the pro-duction advances made by their suppliers. In the 1920s, homes were sheathed with individual boards; now only plywood or OSB is used. Casings for door and window trim were once milled for each home; now trim items are available as stock. Even as late as the 1950s, wire lath and plaster were still used to cover interior panel surfaces and ceilings; now drywall panels are universally used. Indeed, drywall comes in an ever-widening assortment of sizes and compositions to meet special applications.

But further progress is possible, particularly in transforming the home building process into a sequence of subassemblies. For example, more widespread use of

---

5   For a discussion of this difficulty on non-union residential and commercial construction sites, see Lowe, Hagan, and Iskander (2010).

factory-sheathed wall panels would represent an important advance. In interviews for this study, several large home builders stated that they were unable to use wall panels with sheathing preinstalled because of the unevenness of poured foundations. Other respondents reported that they did not use prebuilt wall panels because they were unavailable locally or that it was cheaper to use a local framing crew to build the panels.

A near-term solution to these obstacles seems clear, although it would require fundamental changes to the building process. When dimensional standards are not met at the beginning of the construction process, each subsequent step involves adjustments to compensate for previous errors and compromises the quality of the finished home. Dimensional standards in home building should thus begin with tight but achievable requirements for the flatness of poured concrete foundations. If slab flatness were within at least 1/8 of an inch, home builders would be able to use prebuilt wall panels with sheathing without concerns about racking. Use of factory-built panels not only reduces framing costs but also achieves a level of accuracy for window openings and individual room dimensions rarely seen in site-built homes.

If no wall panel plant exists in a given area, home builders, their framing contractors, and/or the building product supplier can explore options for off-site production of these components. Roof trusses are rarely built on the job site but rather delivered from a local factory, generally a lumberyard or specialized truss plant. Encouraging truss builders to expand into building and sheathing wall panels would therefore be a logical next step.

Placing factory-built panels on a level foundation gets home building off to a rapid start. Such homes can be weather-tight—with roofing in place, outside panels house wrapped, and windows installed—within two days. In some cases, suppliers could provide panels and other major components installed, emulating the modular subassemblies found in the aerospace and automobile industries.

With their expertise in building specific types of subassemblies, these suppliers could work with home builders to co-design major components for different segments of the industry. A firm in the Greater Boston area has recently done precisely this by building modular bathrooms—fully tiled and equipped with electrical and plumbing fixtures—that are shipped to hotels, hospitals, and student and military dormitories as a complete subassembly (Eggrock 2011). The prebuilt bathrooms can be placed directly on flat slab floors without special adjustments to meet slab carpeting. While perhaps no less expensive than site-built bathrooms, these factory-built subassemblies save builders' time and minimize on-site inventory of expensive items.

Progress has also occurred in the areas of HVAC, plumbing, and kitchens. Flexible and thermally pre-insulated ductwork, which distributes conditioned air to each room in the house, is made off-site at a subcontractor's shop and placed in the home before the ceiling wallboard is installed. Plumbing for baths and kitchens can now be connected quickly using braided stainless steel flex connectors of appropriate diameter and length for any plumbing connection.

Home construction could easily approach the sophistication of automobile assembly, where workers no longer use the files and hammers of craftsmen of old. As on the assembly line where well-fitting parts are fastened in place, a home building site could be primarily a place to fasten prebuilt components. Saws would rarely, if ever, be needed to cut pieces to fit. And just as in the auto industry, wider use of preassembly has the further advantage of reducing the necessary skill level of the installation crew.

LEVERAGE THE POWER OF INFORMATION TECHNOLOGY

The Nobel laureate Robert Solow, an economist at MIT, famously quipped in 1987, "You can see the computer age everywhere but in the productivity statistics." This productivity paradox changed radically in the latter 1990s and early 2000s as businesses in a variety of industries learned how to integrate the vast and growing data available via information technologies into new product development, logistics, and inventory control (Fernald and Ramnath 2003; Gordon 2000; Jorgenson 2001; Stiroh 2002). As noted elsewhere, these advances enabled industries like automobiles, retailing, and computers to change the way they performed traditional activities. But they also allowed the creation of new businesses as well as new opportunities for existing businesses. For example, UPS was able to expand beyond its product delivery services to develop a multibillion-dollar division that performs customer service activities for its client companies.

More recently, evolution of the Internet—often referred to as Web 2.0—and related transformations of digital communication devices, such as smartphones, allow businesses to change how products are designed and customized, quickly responding to shifting consumer tastes, such as by adapting to a variety of tastes of those in the "long tail" of demand distributions (Anderson 2006). For example, smartphone application developers constantly create new opportunities to collect information about consumer preferences, past purchases, or even current geographic location that can be used by businesses up and down the supply chains of different industries.

Application to home building. Although computer software had taken over most office functions by the mid-2000s, its penetration into the home building industry—in particular, for cost estimating, scheduling, and communicating with subcontractors and homebuyers—was still limited. For example, at the time of Harvard Home Builder Survey in 2005, it was possible to translate a CAD drawing of a home into a detailed estimate of construction costs based on local prices of building products. If the projected cost met the builder's target price, the design could be transmitted directly to the panel plant over the Internet. If the cost was too high, the design could be reworked until the target as-built price was met. Nevertheless, few survey respondents had fully integrated cost estimation software into their operations by that year. In fact, many did not even use computers to estimate the costs of building a given home design.

Moreover, few home builders used EDI to conduct business-to-business transactions, specialized software to schedule suppliers and subcontractors, or computers to perform back-office functions such as accounting and payroll. Builder divisions operating in lower-appreciation markets, however, were the exception. At the time of the survey, buyers in those locations were clearly price-conscious and builders had to be as productive as possible to ensure a respectable profit margin. One of the many steps they took was to use computers and the Internet to coordinate with subcontractors far more commonly than firms working in higher-appreciation (and higher gross margin) regions of the country.

The case that information and communication technology increases productivity is clear provided that complementary investments are made in people and systems, including reorganization of many management functions (Brynjolfsson and Hitt 2000; Ichniowski et al. 2000). While change in procedures is difficult, expensive, and often painful, home builders now have a compelling opportunity to prepare for the cyclical upturn by updating their ICT systems.

The path to modern communications is well established. A first step would be to develop and implement an integrated information system across all divisions (i.e., a corporate and local area network). This would vastly improve communications inside the company as well as with building product suppliers, subcontractors, and customers. Moreover, the supply of software engineers, programmers, and system integrators to undertake this task has rarely been more plentiful.

Web-based scheduling software used for multi-company coordination and product development could also be directly applied to major home building projects, providing subcontractors with real-time information for planning purposes.[6] The rapidly falling prices of mobile communications, along with expanding wireless coverage, make integrating software-based scheduling systems with smartphones and other PDA/telecommunication devices completely feasible. Many of these systems have already been adopted for major industrial and commercial construction projects. Providing subcontractors real-time, accurate reports on building status would not only reduce transportation time and costs, but also overall construction costs and cycle times.

STREAMLINE SUPPLY CHAIN MANAGEMENT AND LOGISTICS

Two leaders in the automotive and retail industries, Toyota and Walmart, are noted for driving improvements in their supply chains. Toyota is justly famous for developing the idea of parts arriving "just in time" for assembly, whether coming from their own plants or from other suppliers. The company's financial heft is sufficient to ensure compliance with the jointly developed supply plans. Toyota shares its production plans with suppliers well in advance, along with the hourly needs at each plant so that suppliers can provide the parts minutes before assembly. If a defect in a part is found, only a small finished goods inventory requires rework.

Walmart's example illustrates what can be achieved by applying advanced information technology to supply chain management. In essence, Walmart uses computer

---

6   Indicative of the growth in demand of this type of software system was the widely anticipated IPO in December 2007 of Net Suite, which produces accounting software for managing operations within and between businesses. The IPO was viewed as one of the hottest new companies to be taken public since Google. For discussion, see Flynn 2007.

sales records to calculate inventories of every product in every store on a daily basis. Each product is uniquely identified by its UPC bar code, and this information is recorded with each sale. When more products are needed to avoid projected stock-outs, items are ordered automatically and directly from the manufacturers. Corporate Walmart always knows the quantity of all store orders, providing the company a collective presence with suppliers.

Walmart's computers communicate directly with suppliers' computers using EDI to place new orders. Each store's detailed list of requested products is packed in a separate carton, with coded shipping labels indicating the logistical path from manufacturer to store. Computer-to-computer transmission of business data in a standard format has replaced paper documents. This system also avoids ambiguous product descriptions because each product has a unique bar code.

Today most retailers use their own versions of the inventory and ordering systems that Walmart pioneered in 1987, greatly reducing supply chain errors. EDI has led to dramatic reductions in inventory and associated costs. The scale of what has been accomplished is staggering. For example, Macy's in New York City carries several million items as well as many units of each item. Computer systems provide a real-time snapshot of the inventory of each unsold item. Using these supply chain management practices, lean retailers have been able to better match consumer demand and dramatically reduce risk.

Application to home building. Responses to the Harvard Home Builder Survey clearly indicate that many builders operating in lower-appreciation markets often purchased their materials directly from building product suppliers, while firms operating in higher-appreciation markets often left the purchase and installation of products to subcontractors. The latter practice generally diminishes the leverage that larger builders have in negotiating prices and services with suppliers.[7]

The builder is more likely than any subcontractor to be aware of the detailed status of homes at a given site. In principle, then, the builder should schedule the delivery of building products. As discussed in Chapter 5, building materials dealers have adopted advanced supply chain practices, partly in response to consolidation of the overall home building industry. Nevertheless, many builders have not taken advantage of their suppliers' capabilities. This represents a major missed opportunity. By broadly adopting the practices that are now well established in the supply chain serving big-box retailers (The Home Depot and Lowe's), builders and suppliers could dramatically reduce the costs and risks arising from inefficient materials management.

MANAGING RISK IN THE TWENTY-FIRST CENTURY

Risk is a well-known feature of residential construction. Every housing downturn is inevitably followed by declarations from home builders that they will never again be

---

7   Subcontractors working for several large-scale builders may, however, have greater purchasing power with suppliers of products produced locally, such as drywall. Even so, it would appear that corporate-level contracts with manufacturers of branded products, such as windows, would yield cost savings for builders.

caught holding so much land or so many unsold homes. And to their credit in this latest cycle, large home builders did attempt to manage their risks more carefully through the use of land options, land-related joint ventures, and other methods of balancing the need to hold land for future development. Similarly, preselling a larger share of homes was a widely used practice to moderate the risk of what other sectors refer to as "finished goods inventories."

Risk is a fundamental challenge in virtually all industries. The revolution in the financial services industry over the last 25 years involved finding new methods to allow capital markets to improve risk management (Bernstein 2007). Options ideas have also been applied in industries such as energy and pharmaceuticals to hedge risks in analogous ways (Amram and Kulatilaka 2001). While the 2008–9 recession and the unraveling of capital markets—particularly those portions tied to subprime mortgages, highly complex derivatives, and other risk-related strategies— have raised concerns about certain practices, options and other risk management techniques should remain a useful feature of capital markets dealing with mortgage finance (Engel and McCoy 2011).

Yet the length and depth of the economic slump, the erosion of home builders' stock prices, and the problems that continue to plague this volatile industry suggest that large companies still have a long way to go in reducing their risk exposure. Although they will never be able to completely smooth the business cycle or perfectly predict future trends, adopting many of the practices discussed here would help significantly.

While it is impossible for home builders to eliminate the recurring problem of overproduction, strategic use of information technology would dramatically reduce their risk by providing real-time data on demand and then translating that data into information to guide inventory, ordering, pricing, and other critical decisions. Similarly, sharing building plans and schedules with suppliers would allow businesses up and down the supply chain to adjust production decisions in line with demand, thereby reducing the chance of stock-outs and lost sales on the one hand, and excess inventory and the need for markdowns on the other. Implementation of modular assembly, just-in-time production and inventory policies, and innovative human resource practices would provide additional opportunities for home builders to adjust supply to demand more effectively.

The preceding chapters have shown that builders—particularly in divisions that faced tougher market conditions—did experiment with new processes during the housing boom years. The challenges and difficulties of the Great Recession have no doubt encouraged further experimentation. Indeed, the decentralized nature of residential construction affords unique opportunities to try different strategies and, where successful, to diffuse them more broadly. Only with such experimentation and innovation can bigger home builders expect their scale to result in better performance, especially in terms of on-site operations.

This point gets back to the fundamental lesson to be learned from other industries and from the Harvard Home Builder Study. The only way to capture the benefits of the virtuous circle and transform being big into being better is to actively manage and coordinate best practices across all builder divisions. This means breaking from many of the entrenched practices in everything from the conduct of back-office functions, management of construction sites, ordering of building supplies, sourcing of materials and subassemblies, and collection and sharing of information.

If past is prologue, it will be challenging to achieve these fundamental changes. But the fact remains that there has never been a more important moment to learn from the innovative practices in other industries as well as from the residential sector itself. Other manufacturing industries have successfully experimented with advanced approaches and refined their operations over time. While the aftermath of the Great Recession continues to challenge the housing industry, builders can take advantage of this downturn to make significant improvements in their practices. If home builders learn from the problems of the past, they can look to a more promising future.

APPENDIX A

JOINT CENTER ADVISORY PANEL FOR THE HARVARD HOME BUILDER STUDY

CHAIR

Barbara T. Alexander
Senior Advisor
UBS WARBURG

DEALERS/DISTRIBUTORS

Fenton Hord
President and CEO
STOCK BUILDING SUPPLY

Paul W. Hylbert
President and CEO
LANOGA CORPORATION

Michael A. Lupo
President and CEO
HUTTIG BUILDING PRODUCTS, INC.

Frederick Marino
Chairman and CEO
THE STROBER ORGANIZATION, INC.

Robert Mellor
President and CEO
BUILDING MATERIALS
HOLDING CORPORATION

Kevin O'Meara
Senior Vice President –
Operations and COO
BUILDERS FIRSTSOURCE

Lee Thomas
President and COO
GEORGIA-PACIFIC CORPORATION

MANUFACTURERS

William Collins
President and CEO
GAF MATERIALS CORPORATION

Peter Dachowski
Executive Vice President
CERTAINTEED CORPORATION

Karen Mendelsohn
Vice President – Sales and Marketing
MASCO CORPORATION

BUILDERS/REMODELERS

Daniel Fulton
President and CEO
WEYERHAEUSER REAL ESTATE COMPANY

Andy Hannigan
Chairman and CEO
CENTEX HOMES

Isaac Heimbinder
Vice Chairman, President and COO
KIMBALL HILL HOMES

Ken Klein
President
KLEINCO CONSTRUCTION SERVICES, INC.

Ian McCarthy
President and CEO
BEAZER HOMES USA, INC.

Stuart Miller
President and CEO
LENNAR CORPORATION

Bill Owens
President
OWENS CONSTRUCTION
CONTRACTING CO.

MEDIA

Frank Anton
President
HANLEY WOOD, LLC

APPENDIX B

SURVEY RESPONSES TO ICT QUESTIONS

Responses to the corporate survey developed for the Harvard Home Builder Study came from 41 home builder corporations. Many national home builders had several of their divisions participate in the survey, yielding a total of 88 unique responses to the divisional questionnaire. The survey initially asked respondents to describe the general geographic region (Northeast, Midwest, Southeast, Southwest, or West) served by their offices. After preliminary examination of results, however, the research team found that the specific metropolitan area served by each division was likely to be an important variable in understanding builder performance.

Each divisional survey respondent was then contacted to obtain this information. In this way, the specific location served by 73 of the 88 divisions was identified. Several respondents reported that they were regional divisions serving multiple metropolitan areas, while others operated in areas outside of standard metro areas. In the end, only 62 divisions were identified as serving a single metropolitan statistical area (MSA) as defined by the US Census Bureau.

This means that if every division operating in an identified metropolitan area answered a particular ICT question, the maximum number of possible responses would be 62. But if all builder divisions answered, the maximum number would be 88 (including the 62 divisions operating in known metro areas). In Chapter 6, all tables reporting the responses of divisions operating in MSAs with lower and higher home price appreciation include a column listing the responses from all divisions answering the particular question.

As in Chapter 5 on advanced operational practices, the metro area where each division was actively building homes in 2004 was the parameter used to sort the responses of the ICT sections of the survey into two distinct groups: one of the divisions operating in metro areas with less than 60 percent appreciation in home prices from 1999–2004, and the other of divisions operating in metro areas with 60 percent or more appreciation in home prices. By sorting the responses in this way, it was possible to test if the advanced supply chain management practices among builders operating in lower-appreciation markets might carry over to more extensive use of ICT.

Divisional responses to each question were also analyzed by the size of the parent corporation. For purposes of the ICT chapter, divisions were sorted into three subgroups of nearly equal size: those with parent companies selling fewer than 2,500 homes in 2004 (26 divisions); those with parent companies selling between 2,500 and 9,999 homes (27 divisions); and those with parent companies selling 10,000 or more homes (35 divisions). The last group of corporations comprises the so-called national builders. Sorting the responses into these subgroups made it possible to explore how the scale of the parent company influenced divisional use of a particular item or form of ICT.

REFERENCES

Abernathy, Frederick H., John T. Dunlop, Janice H. Hammond, and David Weil. 1999. *A stitch in time: Lean retailing and the transformation of manufacturing*. New York: Oxford University Press.

Abernathy, Frederick H., John T. Dunlop, David Weil, William Apgar, Kermit Baker, and Rachel Roth. 2004. Residential supply chain in transition: Summary of findings from survey of dealers. Working paper. Cambridge, MA: Joint Center for Housing Studies of Harvard University.

Ahluwalia, Gopal. 2003. Subcontracting and channels of distribution. *Housing Economics* 5:7–12.

Amram, Martha, and Nalin Kulatilaka. 2001. *Real options: Managing strategic investment in an uncertain world*. Boston, MA: Harvard Business School Press.

Anderson, Chris. 2006. *The long tail: Why the future of business is selling less of more*. New York, NY: Hyperion.

Appelbaum, Eileen, and Rosemary Batt. 1995. *The new American workplace: Transforming work systems in the United States*. Ithaca, NY: Cornell University Press.

Arlen, Jennifer, and W. Bentley MacLeod. 2005. Beyond master-servant: A critique of vicarious liability. In *Exploring Tort Law*, Stuart Madden, ed. New York: Cambridge University Press.

Beazer Homes. 1997. *Going places*. Annual report. Atlanta, GA: Beazer Homes USA, Inc. www.proquest.com.

———. 2004. *It's what's inside that counts*. Annual report. Atlanta, GA: Beazer Homes USA, Inc. www.proquest.com.

Bernhardt, Annette, Ruth Milkman, Nik Theodore, Douglas Heckathorn, Mirabei Auer, James DeFillipis, Ana Luz Gonzalez, Victor Narro, Jason Perelshteyn, Diana Polson, and Michael Spiller. 2009. *Broken laws, unprotected workers: Violations of employment in labor laws in America's cities*. Center for Urban Economic Development, University of Illinois Chicago; National Employment Law Project; UCLA Institute for Research on Labor and Employment.

Bernstein, Peter. 2007. *Capital ideas evolving.* Hoboken, NJ: John Wiley & Sons, Inc.

Bordenaro, Michael. 2005. Blue sky scenario. *Big Builder,* May 1.

Brown, Stephen. 1997. *Revolution at the check-out counter: The explosion of the bar code.* Cambridge, MA: Harvard Wertheim Publications Committee/Harvard University Press.

Brynjolfsson, Erik, and Lorin M. Hitt. 2000. Beyond computation: Information technology, organizational transformation and business performance. *Journal of Economic Perspectives* 14:4, 23–48.

Carliner, Michael. 2001. Housing and GDP. *Housing Economics* 10:7–9.

———. 2003a. Builders' computer use. *Housing Economics* 12:8–10.

———. 2003b. New home cost components. *Housing Economics* 3:8–11.

———. 2005. Home building industry. Presentation to the Construction Economics Research Network. Silver Spring, MD: NAHB Economics and Research Department.

Chandler, Alfred D. 1990. *Scale and scope: The dynamics of industrial capitalism.* Cambridge, MA: Harvard University Press.

Cohan, William. 2009. *House of cards: A tale of hubris and wretched excess on Wall Street.* New York: Doubleday.

Commons, John R. 1904. The New York building trades. *The Quarterly Journal of Economics* 18(3):409–36.

Congressional Budget Office. 1993. *Resolving the thrift crisis. A CBO study.* Washington, DC: Congressional Budget Office.

DeCain, Paul. 2002. *The impending consolidation of the homebuilding industry.* New York: Andersen Corporate Finance.

D.R. Horton. 1996. *Annual report.* Arlington, TX: D.R. Horton Custom Homes. www.proquest.com.

———. 2004. *Annual report.* Fort Worth, TX: D.R. Horton Custom Homes. www.proquest.com.

Dunlop, John T. 1961. The industrial relations system in construction. In *The structure of collective bargaining,* Arnold Weber, ed. Chicago: University of Chicago Press.

———. 1993. *Industrial relations systems.* Revised edition. Cambridge, MA: Harvard Business School Press Classic.

Eccles, Robert. 1981. The quasi-firm in the construction industry. *Journal of Economic Behavior and Organization* 2, 335–57.

Eggrock. 2011. www.eggrock.com/index.html.

Engel, Kathleen, and Patricia McCoy. 2011. *The subprime virus: Reckless credit, regulatory failure, and next steps.* New York: Oxford University Press.

eTForecasts. 2011. *Worldwide PC market.* www.etforecasts.com/products/ES_pcww1203.htm.

Fernald, John, and Shanthi Ramnath. 2003. Information technology and the US productivity acceleration. *Chicago Fed Letter* 193, September.

Flynn, Laurie. 2007. Going public caps dream for a maker of software. *New York Times,* December 18: C1, C2.

Gerardi, Kristopher, Adam Hale Shapiro, and Paul S. Willen. 2007. *Subprime outcomes: Risky mortgages, homeownership experiences, and foreclosures.* Working Paper 07-15. Boston, MA: Federal Reserve Bank of Boston.

Gordon, Robert J. 2000. Does the "new economy" measure up to the great inventions of the past? *Journal of Economic Perspectives* 14(4):49–74.

Gramlich, Edward. 2007. Booms and busts: The case of subprime mortgages. *Economic Review,* Fourth Quarter. Federal Reserve Bank of Kansas City.

Greenhouse, Steven. 2008. *The big squeeze: Tough times for the American worker.* New York: Alfred A. Knopf.

Grist, Peter. 2010. *Housing and GDP.* Special studies. National Association of Home Builders. www.nahb.org/generic.aspx?genericContentID=136170.

Group of Twenty Finance Ministers and Central Bank Governors. 2008. *Declaration of the summit on financial markets and the world economy.* White House press release, November 15. http://georgewbush-whitehouse.archives.gov/news/releases.

Haas, Carl T., John D. Borcherding, Eric Allmon, and Paul M. Goodrum. 1999. US construction labor productivity trends, 1970–1998. Report no.7. Austin, Texas: Center for Construction Industry Studies, The University of Texas at Austin.

Haberman, Alan, ed. 2001. *Twenty-five years behind bars.* Cambridge, MA: Harvard Wertheim Publications Committee/Harvard University Press

Hale, Peter. 2009. *Levittown: Documents of an ideal American suburb.* Chicago: Art History Department, University of Illinois. http://tigger.uic.edu/~pbhales/Levittown.html.

Hanley Wood Market Intelligence. 2004. *Builder* magazine, Local Leaders list.

Ichniowski, Casey, David Levine, and Craig Olson, eds. 2000. *The American workplace: Skills, compensation, and employee involvement.* Cambridge, UK: Cambridge University Press.

Immergluck, Daniel. 2009. *Foreclosed: High-risk lending, deregulation, and the undermining of America's mortgage market.* Ithaca: Cornell University Press.

Inside Mortgage Finance. 2009. *Mortgage market statistical annual.* Bethesda, MD: Inside Mortgage Finance Publications.

Internet World Stats. 2011. *Internet world stats blog, July 1–December 31, 2004.* www. internetworldstats.com/blog2.htm.

Iskander, Natasha, Nicola Lowe, and Christine Riordan. 2009. The rise and fall of a micro-learning region: Mexican immigrants and construction in South-Center Philadelphia, 2000–2009. NYU Wagner research paper. New York, NY: New York University.

Johnson, Kirk. 2007. A $135 million home, but if you have to ask... *New York Times,* July 2: A1.

Jorgenson, Dale W. 2001. Information technology and the US economy. *American Economic Review* 90:1, 1–32.

Keller, Kevin. 2008. *Strategic brand management: Building, measuring, and managing brand equity*. 3rd edition. Upper Saddle River, NJ: Pearson/Prentice Hall.

Kochhar, Rakesh. 2006. *Growth in the foreign-born workforce and employment of the native born*. Washington, DC: Pew Hispanic Center.

Koebel, C. Theodore, and Marilyn Cavell. 2006. *Characteristics of innovative production home builders*. Blacksburg, VA: Virginia Center for Housing Research, Virginia Polytechnic Institute.

Krugman, Paul. 2005. Greenspan and the bubble. *New York Times,* April 29.

Lazonick, William. 2009. Sustainable prosperity in the new economy? *Business organization and high-tech employment in the United States*. Kalamazoo, MI: Upjohn Institute for Employment Research.

Lewis, Michael. 2010. *The big short: Inside the doomsday machine*. New York: W.W. Norton & Co.

Lowe, Nichola, Jacqueline Hagan, and Natasha Iskander. 2010. Revealing talent: Informal skills intermediation as an emergent pathway to immigrant labor market incorporation. *Environment and Planning A,* 42(1) 205–222.

MacDuffie, John Paul, and Susan Helper. 1997. Creating lean suppliers: Diffusing lean production through the supply chain. *California Management Review* 39(4):118–51.

McLean, Bethany and Joe Nocera. 2010. *All the devils are here: The hidden history of the financial crisis*. New York: Portfolio/Penguin.

Moody's Investors Service. 2006. *US homebuilding land options and joint ventures: Hidden in plain sight?* Special comment, August. http://ssrn.com/abstract=979813.

Morris, Charles R. 2008. *The trillion dollar meltdown: Easy money, high rollers, and the great credit crash*. New York: PublicAffairs.

Pendall, Rolf, Robert Puentes, and Jonathan Martin. 2006. *From traditional to reformed: A review of the land use regulations in the nation's 50 largest metropolitan areas*. Washington, DC: The Brookings Institution.

Penrose, Edith T. 1995. *The theory of the growth of the firm*. 3rd edition. New York: Oxford University Press.

Pfeffer, Jeffrey. 1998. *The human equation: Building profits by putting people first*. Boston, MA: Harvard Business School Press.

Pil, Frits K., and John Paul MacDuffie. 1996. The adoption of high involvement work practices. *Industrial Relations* 35(3):423–55.

Porter, Michael E. 2003. *The US homebuilding industry and the competitive position of large builders*. Presentation at the Centex Investor Conference, New York, NY, November 18.

Quigley, John, and Larry Rosenthal. 2005. The effects of land use regulation on the price of housing: What do we know? What can we learn? *Cityscape* 8(1):69–116.

Shiller, Robert J. 2008. *The subprime solution: How today's global financial crisis happened, and what to do about it*. Princeton: Princeton University Press.

Shulman, Beth. 2003. *The betrayal of work: How low-wage jobs fail 30 million Americans.* New York: New Press.

Sloan, Alfred P. 1963. *My years with General Motors.* New York: Doubleday.

Solow, Robert. 1987. We'd better watch out. *New York Times Book Review,* July 12, 36.

Sorkin, Andrew Ross. 2009. *Too big to fail: The inside story of how Wall Street and Washington fought to save the financial system from crisis—and themselves.* New York: Viking.

Steven Winter Associates, Inc. 2005. *Integrating panels into the production homebuilding process.* Report prepared for US Department of Housing and Urban Development.

Stiroh, Kevin J. 2002. Information technology and the US productivity revival: What do the industry data say? *The American Economic Review* 92(5):1559–76.

Taylor, John, and Hans Bjornsson. 2002. Identification and classification of value drivers for a new production homebuilding supply chain. *Proceedings of the International Group for Lean Construction*–10, Gramado, Brazil, 1–12.

Teicholz, Paul. 2004. Labor productivity declines in the construction industry: Causes and remedies. *AECbytes*, Viewpoint #4, April14.

UBS Investment Bank. 2008. Custom tabulations prepared for the Joint Center for Housing Studies of Harvard University.

US Census Bureau. 2010. Families and living arrangements, historical time series, table HH-1. households, by type: 1940 to present. www.census.gov/population/socdemo/hh-fam/hh1.xls.

US Department of Commerce, Bureau of Economic Analysis. 2011. Gross domestic product. http://research.stlouisfed.org/fred2/data/GDPC1.txt.

US Department of Labor, Bureau of Labor Statistics. 2008. Current Employment Statistics survey.

Weil, David. 2005. The contemporary industrial relations system in construction: Analysis, observations, and speculations. *Labor History* 46(4):447–71.

———. 2010. *Improving workplace conditions through strategic enforcement.* Report prepared for the U.S. Department of Labor, Wage and Hour Division.

Wellings, Fred. 2006. *British homebuilders: History and analysis.* Oxford, UK: Blackwell Publishing.

Whelan, Margaret. 2005. *The future of big builders.* Presentation at Hanley Wood's American Housing Conference, September 21.

Womack, James P., Daniel T. Jones, and Daniel Roos. 1991. *The machine that changed the world.* New York: Harper Perennial.

Zandi, Mark. 2009. *Financial shock: A 360° look at the subprime mortgage implosion, and how to avoid the next financial crisis.* Upper Saddle River, NJ: FT Press.

INDEX

construction costs: and advantages of scale, 52–53, 53 (fig. 4.9), 54 (fig. 4.10); and market characteristics, 68, 68 (fig. 5.7)

construction cycle time, 54–56, 55n14; and market characteristics, 68, 68 (fig. 5.7)

construction manager (CM) model, 39–45; costs and benefits, 46–48; and high-road approach, 95–97; modification of, 57; role at construction site, 40–42

construction practices, 39–57

construction site, performance at, 52–56

contracting out, 94

contractors: basic trades, 17, 40, 95; skilled trades, 48, 96–97; specialty trades, 17, 40. *See also* subcontractors

coordination: and ICT use, 78–79; improving, 59; of on-site activities, 48–52; of supply chain management, 88

coordinator role. *See* construction manager (CM) model

corporate branding, 9, 35–38, 73, 91–92

corporate-level survey respondents, 25; results, 27–38

cost estimating: and ICT use, 77–79, 82; software for, 99

craft training, 96–97

customer experience, consistency of, 37–38, 37 (fig. 3.8)

customer satisfaction, 35–38, 91–92

customer support centers, 94

dealer services, enhanced, 63. *See also* pro dealers

debt financing, 8

delivery delays, and labor productivity, 60

Del Webb, 35

Dell Computers, 96–97

Delta Airlines, 72

design of homes, 16

de-verticalization, 94

dimensional standards, in home building, 98

direct employment, 95

divisions, of home builder companies: and advanced operational practices, 69; and EDI use, 74, 74 (fig. 6.1); and improved operations, 62–63, 63 (fig. 5.2); and on-site ICT use, 75–77; size of, and construction cycle time, 55, 56 (fig. 4.12); as survey participants, 23–24, 23 (fig. 2.4), 25–26

Dow Chemical Company, 94n1

D. R. Horton, 7, 37

drywall, 17

e-commerce systems, 81–82, 82 (fig. 6.6). *See also* information and communications technology (ICT)

EDI (Electronic Data Interchange), 74, 83, 99–101

efficiency measures, and advantages of scale, 45, 46 (fig. 4.5)

Eggrock, 98

electrical work, 17, 43

employment: direct, 42–43, 43 (fig. 4.2), 47, 95; fissured, 46, 48; and immigration status, 47, 96; and labor standards violations, 47–48; and vicarious liability, 57n15, 95n3; *See also* labor

energy industries, 102

entry-level homes: construction cycle time for, 54–55, 55 (fig. 4.11); HHBS focus on, 17–19

equity financing, 8; as benefit of scale, 30, 30n1

expansion, big builders and, 31

Federal Housing Finance Agency (FHFA), 19n1

Federal Reserve Board, 3

financial performance, survey respondents and, 25

financial services industry, 94, 102; deregulation, 5

finish work, 17

Ford, Henry, 97

Ford Motor Company, 52, 72, 96–97

foundation, 16

framing, 16–17, 43, 43 (fig. 4.2), 44 (fig. 4.3), 45 (fig. 4.4)

GDP, growth of, 3

general contractor (GC), 40, 40n1

General Electric Company, 94n1, 97

General Motors Corporation, 86n1

Gramlich, Edward, 3

Great Recession, 96, 102–3

Greenspan, Alan, 4

gross margins, 31 (fig. 3.4), 32–33, 86–88

Group of 20, *Declaration of the Summit on Financial Markets and the World Economy,* 4

Hale, Peter, 47n6

Harvard Building Products Distribution Study, 61, 81

Harvard Home Builder Study, 1, 15–22; corporate-level responses, 27–38; survey coverage and content, 23–24; survey respondents, 23–24, 23 (fig. 2.3); survey structure, 24–26

Harvard Joint Center for Housing Studies, Policy Advisory Board, 26

Hewlett Packard, 97

home builders. *See* big builders

home building, sequence of steps in, 15–17

Macy's, 96, 101

management functions, reorganization of, and ICT adoption, 100

manufacturer-direct distribution system, 61

market conditions, as factor in performance, 28

market share, big builders' increases in, 5–7

market type, and construction practices, 39–40

mason contractor, 40, 40n1

mass-production assembly line model, 47n6, 97

master-servant relationship, 57n15, 95n3

materials handling, and advantages of scale, 59–60

materials management, 69

M. D. C. Holdings, 37

metropolitan markets, big builders' market share in, 7, 8 (fig. 1.4)

Microsoft Office for Windows 95 (program), 72

mobile communications, 100

modular bathrooms, 98

modular production, 97

Moody's Investors Service, 32

mortgage securities, collateralization of, 3

multiple sites, management of, 47

National Association of Home Builders (NAHB), 2, 41n3, 60, 86

NCR Corporation, 94n1

Net Suite, 100n6

Newsweek, 72

New York Times, 18, 72

Office of Federal Housing Enterprise Oversight (OFHEO) House Price Index, 19–20, 19n1

operating costs, 8

operational performance, 54–56, 67–69, 68 (fig. 5.7); challenges of improving, 86–88, 87 (fig. 7.1); division-level survey respondents and, 25

operational practices, advanced, 59–69

options. *See* land options

outsourcing, 94

overhead costs, 8

overproduction, 102

Partnership for Advancing Technology in Housing (PATH) program (HUD), 9

performance: and advantages of scale, 85–92; and market characteristics, 67–69, 68 (fig. 5.7); on-site, 52–56. *See also* operational performance

permitting process, 16

personal computer industry, 97

pharmaceuticals industry, 102

plumbing, 17, 43; and use of subassemblies, 98

population growth, U.S., 2–3

portability of skills, 96

Porter, Michael, 9

Power Circle Ratings, 36n4

preassembly of components, 59–60, 64, 97–99

preselling, 102; "presold" agreements, 47n7

pricing programs, corporate, 62–64, 62 (fig. 5.1)

Procter & Gamble, 54

pro dealers, as third supply channel, 60–62

product identification, and ICT, 73

product proliferation, 61

productivity paradox, 99

Professional Builder (magazine), 9

profitability: focus on, 38, 85–86, 91; and size, 9

public companies, big builders as, 7, 30

Pulte, 37; Del Webb (brand of), 35

purchase orders, computerization of, 73–74

purchasing programs, corporate, 62–64

quality control circles, 94

retail industry, 18; and EDI use, 75. *See also* lean retailing

retirement housing, 18

review process, 16

risk management, 101–2; and construction practices, 39; for land holding, 33–34; and subcontractors, 41, 46

Rolls-Royce, 97

roof trusses, 17, 98

Sacramento, California, 21

savings & loan institutions (S&Ls), and borrow short/lend long strategy, 4–5

scale, advantages of, 1, 30; achieving, 93–103; and CM model, 47; conventional wisdom on, 8–10; and efficiency measures, 45, 46 (fig. 4.5); and ICT, 71–72; and performance, 85–92; potential for, 91–92

scheduling information, 50–51, 50 (fig. 4.7), 51 (fig. 4.8), 73

single-family home starts, 2, 2 (fig. 1.1). *See also* entry-level homes

size, of home builder, 25; and construction practices, 39–40; and location, 89–91, 90 (figs. 7.3 and 7.4); and performance, 29–30, 29 (fig. 3.3); and profitability, 9. *See also* scale, advantages of

skills, portability of, 96

SKUs, 61, 73

Sloan, Alfred P., 86n1

smartphones, 99–100

software, 71; cost estimating, 99; Web-based, for scheduling, 100. *See also* information and communications technology (ICT)

Solow, Robert, 99

speculative building, 47, 47n7, 52, 54

standardization: of components, 97–99; of practices, across acquisitions, 59

starter homes. *See* entry-level homes

subassemblies, prebuilt, 97–99

subcontracting: consolidation of subcontractor base, 49–50; division-level survey respondents and, 26; regional variations in practices, 66n2

subcontractor coordination, improving, 94–97

subcontractors, 41–43, 42 (fig. 4.1), 44 (fig. 4.3); awarding work to, 48–49, 49 (fig. 4.6); and CM model, 95–97; and information sharing, 50–52, 51 (fig. 4.8), 78–81, 80 (fig. 6.4), 81 (fig. 6.5); payments to, as builder's largest expense category, 41, 41n3, 42 (fig. 4.1), 52; and purchasing, 66, 66 (fig. 5.5); and share of work, 44

subdivision of land, 41n2; regional variations in, 31–32

subprime lending: growth of, 3–4

suppliers, and information sharing, 78–81, 80 (fig. 6.4), 81 (fig. 6.5)

supply chain management, 60, 64–65, 88; and advantages of scale, 59–60, 91; corporate-level survey respondents and, 25; division-level survey respondents and, 26; and information sharing, 78–81, 80 (fig. 6.4), 81 (fig. 6.5); streamlining, 100–101

Target, 96

team-based production, 94

Toll Brothers luxury homes, 35

tort law, 57n15, 95n3

Toyota, 94, 96–97, 100

"tradeup" homes, 18

training, 95–97, 97n5. *See also* apprenticeship programs

transportation issues, 16

UBS Investment Bank, 30

undocumented workers, 47, 96

United Parcel Service, 99

United Technologies, 97

vicarious liability, 57n15, 95n3

Virginia Tech, Center for Housing Research, 9

virtuous circle, 10–12, 11 (fig. 1.5), 24, 39, 56, 69, 91, 96, 103; and construction costs, 52–53; and construction cycle time, 54–56

wall panels, 98

Walmart, 54, 96, 100–101

Web sites, builders', 72

Wellings, Fred, 10

"willingness to recommend," as standard for customer satisfaction, 36

windows, 17, 63–64, 64 (fig. 5.3)

workforce quality, improving, 94–97

working conditions, and CM model, 47–48

CPSIA information can be obtained at www.ICGtesting.com
Printed in the USA
BVOW022331190212

283213BV00002B/1/P